917.
304
JOH

Johnson, David,
 1947-

No ordinary lives.

DATE			

No
Ordinary
Lives

NO ORDINARY LIVES

One Man's Surprising Journey
into the Heart of America

DAVID JOHNSON

WARNER BOOKS

An AOL Time Warner Company

Warner Books, Inc., 1271 Avenue of the Americas, New York, NY 10020

Visit our Web site at www.twbookmark.com.

 An AOL Time Warner Company

Printed in the United States of America

First Printing: July 2002

10 9 8 7 6 5 4 3 2 1

Library of Congress Cataloging-in-Publication Data
Johnson, David.
    No ordinary lives : one man's surprising journey into the heart of America / David Johnson.
        p. cm.
    ISBN 0-446-52639-8
    1. Idaho—Biography. 2. Washington (State)—Biography. 3. United States—Social life and customs. 4. Johnson, David, 1947– 5. Journalists—Idaho—Biography. I. Title.

CT231 .J64 2002
920.0796—dc21   2001026875

Book design by Giorgetta Bell McRee

For Diane and her mother

Acknowledgments

I've found that making the transition from longtime newspaper reporter to first-time book author can't be done without the help and support of many people.

On the book side, I thank editor Rick Horgan of Warner Books for his expertise and unwavering patience throughout this project. I also extend a literary hug to Jody Handley for her love of words and precocious editing abilities. I am forever indebted to agent David Black for being first to call me with this book idea and then steadfastly standing behind both the project and me. Thanks also to Joy Tutela for giving the book direction and then keeping me on course.

On the newspaper side, I thank publisher A. L. (Butch) Alford, Jr., not only for hiring me more than two decades ago, but also for keeping the *Lewiston Morning Tribune* steeped in journalistic tradition. Former *Tribune* executive editor Jay Shelledy taught me to honor that tradition and pursue stories beyond the obvious news. Thanks to *Tribune*

ACKNOWLEDGMENTS

managing editor Paul Emerson and city editor Diane Pettit for being my bosses and my friends. I'm grateful to all the other editors who handled my copy over the years, including Ted Stanton of the *Daily Idahonian*, the *Tribune*'s Ladd Hamilton, Perry Swisher, Cassandra Tate, Mindy Cameron, Kevin Roche, Jim Godbold, John Killen, and Sandra Lee.

Mostly, I thank the everyday people who continue to tell me their stories. They've made my own story all the richer.

Contents

No
Ordinary
Lives

Preface

Newspaper reporters write about what other people say and do. We hound politicians, chase ambulances, cover murder trials, and otherwise react to current events. In that way, journalism is a time-honored exercise of holding the proverbial mirror up to society.

But about twenty-five years ago, I got an idea to catch the reflection in a different way. Eventually, I turned the idea into a weekly column that still appears on the front page of the *Lewiston Morning Tribune* in Idaho.

Titled "Everyone Has a Story," the column has nothing to do with the news but almost everything to do with life as we routinely live it. While writing the column for the better part of two decades, I've learned some things about people, the world, and even myself.

When I got the idea, I never thought such a thing would happen.

Introduction

The morning had turned into one of those wretchedly wet February afternoons when winter grudgingly gives way to spring. A warm Chinook wind had melted almost all the snow from the plateau country around the tiny town of Cavendish in north central Idaho. The two-day gale left the road in front of the town's only store pocked with puddles. A bank of spent storm clouds sparred with the sun on the western horizon.

I pulled the car over, parked, grabbed my notebook and camera, and shoved open the store's stubborn door. A tiny bell announced my arrival.

"Are you open?" I asked, spotting a plaid-shirted man in suspenders.

"Sure are. Come on in," said Leo Koch, tipping a leather visor up from his forehead to reveal welcoming eyes. "We're always open."

He held a miniature meat cleaver in one hand and a chunk of cheddar in the other, and he wore a toothless grin on his granddad face.

"Darn good cheese," said Leo, slicing a wafer-thin portion onto a wooden cutting board. "Here, try some."

"Well, okay." I pinched the offering between my thumb and finger, chewed twice, and swallowed.

"Thanks."

"You bet."

There were nineteen chunks of Tillamook in the cooler in the back of the Cavendish Store. If all the people in town bought a block, Leo calculated, there'd be two chunks left.

"But, oh, I made a good profit so far today," he jested, sorting through a hollow-sounding cash-register drawer where some food stamps and six dollars in assorted change hid. "Sold a candy bar and a loaf of bread, and one guy aired-up his truck tires." Leo speculated that he might even double his take by the time the sun went down. Resigned to long hours with little to show for it, he eased himself into a captain's chair over by the soup cans and opened the newspaper to the obituaries.

"Take your time. Let me know when you need some help."

I shuffled down one aisle of the old store and up another as the floor creaked beneath my feet. The ceiling was high, the walls were in need of paint, and the inventory was lacking. Two bare lightbulbs hung down from long cords and glowed like holes in the dusk of a bygone day. I snatched a Milky Way from the candy shelf and a cola from the cooler that also housed the cheese.

"Hey, um, my name is Dave Johnson. I'm a reporter for the *Daily Idahonian*."

"Johnson. That sounds like a good Swede name."

"Ya. Minnesotan," I quipped.

"Ya, I'm from Minnesota myself," said Leo, taking a second glance at me over the newspaper. "Born in Park Rapids."

"I know the place."

"Went to school in Arago."

"Never heard of it."

"You never heard of Cavendish, either, I bet."

Actually, I *had* heard of Cavendish. But I'd never before visited the little hamlet, which served as a welcome mat to Idaho's mountains farther east. Half a dozen homes and a log church widened the road alongside Leo's false-front store.

"So Leo, how do you pronounce your last name?" I asked.

"Koch. The same as that young fella who just won the silver medal over there in the Olympics. Boy, he's some-thin'."

On the other side of the world in Innsbruck, where the 1976 Winter Olympics were taking place, American cross-country skier Bill Koch had thrilled the nation two days earlier with his second-place finish in the thirty-kilometer Nordic race. The radio, in fact, was still trumpeting young Koch's performance when I stopped at the Cavendish Store and found Leo.

"Any relation?" I asked.

"Naa," said Leo, his smile disappearing behind the news-paper again.

I'd been working for five months as a general assignment reporter for a small afternoon newspaper in Moscow, Idaho, and seldom ventured out of the paper's circulation area. But on this day, I fell victim to the siren-like quality of the distant Cavendish plateau. It lured me down the Kendrick Grade on Highway 3, back up the other side of the breaks along Potlatch Creek, through the time-worn skeletal farming towns of Cameron and Southwick near the head-waters of Bedrock Creek, and on to the next semi-wide spot in a county road where the sign in Leo's store read: *Sure, we're open.*

Leo owned the store along with his wife, and he lamented that their business was all but dead. Not too many years earlier, there'd been a grocery three miles away and another in Southwick that offered competition. But the bigger farms had swallowed the smaller farms, people started moving to the city, and business suffered.

"That's the way it goes." Leo shrugged. "Us old folks are goin' to fade away like old soldiers."

I put my candy bar and pop down near the cash register and walked back over to where Leo was sitting with his newspaper.

"Has anybody ever interviewed you?" I asked.

"Nope."

"Well, how about if I ask you some questions about this place—you know, about Cavendish and your store here and some of the history?"

There was no news in Cavendish; nothing that begged to be told or rose to the level of the public's right to know. But my reporter's instinct hinted at something intriguing below the surface.

"If you're planning to get some of the stories around this country, you'd better hurry. Not many people left."

I glanced at a straight-backed wooden chair and Leo nodded for me to sit down. I eased my notebook out of my back pants pocket, pulled one of three pens out of my shirt, and let the camera slip off my shoulder. "How old are you?"

Leo lowered his newspaper, leaned back in the captain's chair, and answered, "Seventy-one." With little need for additional questions, he began to talk, coaxing history out of the store's silent corners. There was a day, he said, when half the shop was lined with horse collars, tack, and hardware and the other half with life's essentials.

"Guys used to sit around the stove tellin' stories as tall as could be," said Leo. The store became such a hub of activity that he had to refinish the floor twice where the storytellers' rocking chairs wore holes in the wood.

"Used to be more people all over, but they retired or moved out. Cavendish used to have a lot more umph," lamented Leo. "Now it's not even listed in the phone book."

I stopped writing notes as a gust of wind brushed against the building.

"What was that? What did you say, something about the phone book?"

Leo shrugged, as if whatever he'd said hadn't mattered, and continued to talk of his store and how times had changed.

"Up until a few years ago, it took us two trips a week to Lewiston to keep the store supplied. Now we go maybe once a week and . . ."

I'm not sure if the idea hit me at that moment, later in the interview, on the way home, or sometime after Leo's story ran on the front page. It was all so long ago. But in my mind, I often revisit that day with Leo in the Cavendish Store. It was a defining moment in my newspaper career. I began to realize, while sitting there amid the soup cans and small talk, that some of the best stories—the kind that go beyond simple news to touch all that's human—are right there in front of us.

What's more, the people who can tell them are listed, of all places, in the telephone book.

"Everyone has a story," whispered a voice inside my head.

CHAPTER ONE

Putting Legs on a Notion

To be honest, the idea that everyone has a story worth telling was probably lurking in me long before I met Leo Koch; maybe as far back as 1972 when I entered journalism school at the University of Idaho and found myself in over my head. Hard news reporters, the kind who feast on breaking stories and scour the depths of complicated issues, are products of journalistic tradition. They seek the highs that come with finding scoops and beating deadlines.

I'm more a product of coincidence and two-finger typing. Thinking back, I can still hear the old Underwood as I concealed myself toward the rear of my first University of Idaho reporting class.

Tap-tap. Tap-tap-tap.

I was pecking away on my biography. It was my first assignment and, among the dozen or so students in class, I was finishing last.

Tap-tap. Tap.

Not that I had that much to say about my modest life of twenty-four years. I just couldn't type very fast. In fact, the assignment was supposed to be a one-pager.

"Just write something about yourself as an introduction to the rest of the class," the instructor said.

University of Idaho journalism classes back then were held in a gunboat gray two-room building whose ceilings showered fine particles of dust whenever the typewriters began pounding. As the dust cascaded around me, I blissfully focused on the part about my being from Minnesota.

Tap-tap-tap. Tap . . .

I looked up from my debut effort and caught the glance of classmate Rick Ripley, who would eventually become a reporter for the Associated Press. Nearby sat Bill Fitzgerald, who was destined to leap over his journalism career and become a lawyer. Both were politely peering back over their shoulders to see who was about to miss his first deadline.

"Howdy," I'd written. "I'm Dave Johnson from Fridley, Minnesota. I moved here two weeks ago because I flunked my army draft physical due to high blood pressure and somebody said they'd give me a $300 scholarship if I came to the University of Idaho and combined a degree in journalism with the one I already have in wildlife management from the University of Minnesota."

I was proud of my wildlife degree. Believe it or not, back then my career fantasy was to count and manage ducks—and then write about counting and managing ducks. While getting my bachelor's at Minnesota, I became fascinated with waterfowl and worked the summer of 1969 on a duck-banding crew for the state conservation department. One day, while my crew members and I were up to our armpits in a slough near Fergus Falls chasing molting mallards, we were paid a visit by an outdoor reporter from the *Minneapolis Star* named Ron Shara.

"So tell me about your job," Shara asked from the dry edge of the pond we were working. He wore a safari-type shirt and what appeared to be brand-new hip boots, and generally affected a coiffed, outdoorsy look.

"Well," I said, "we wade around in here, scare all the ducks into a net, catch 'em, band 'em, and then let 'em go again."

Shara wrote all that down and a photographer took a picture as I released a "flapper" back to the wild. My hand, with the duck just taking flight, appeared in the Sunday *Star*.

When I read Shara's story about a week later, I thought, Heck, I can do that! Writing about somebody being up to his armpits in a slough seemed more sensible than actually doing it. I also figured it was more lucrative, although today I'm not sure about that.

Anyway, with a Vietnam tour not in the cards as it was for so many young men, I came to Idaho with my first wife, plugged away on the old Underwood for eighteen months, and graduated from journalism school about the time the Watergate scandal was heating up. Everyone in my class, it seemed, wanted to be an investigative reporter like those two guys from the *Washington Post*.

But not me. I showed little interest in politics, breaking news, or the competition that real newspaper reporters craved. So I got an entry-level job in public information at the University of Idaho College of Forestry, Wildlife and Range Sciences, and turned out news releases about research projects. The work put me in touch with a variety of interesting animal species and the equally intriguing people who studied them. I couldn't wait for the next writing adventure. I was consumed by the challenge and harbored dreams of someday working for *Field & Stream* or some other outdoor magazine.

Then one cold Friday evening just before Christmas of 1974, whatever outdoor writing ambitions I may have had became a casualty of my unraveling personal life. In the living room of a house where laughter was no longer heard, I gently embraced my wife of five years and asked, "Why don't we love each other anymore?" It was a flawed question. I hadn't fallen out of love. But I knew *she* had. I could feel it in our one-sided embrace.

"I don't know," she whispered, burying her head in my chest and then pulling me closer than she had in months. "I don't know." We had been high school sweethearts in the northern suburbs of Minneapolis. She had been the 1965 homecoming queen at Fridley High School and I'd been the football captain. Four years after graduation, we had a church wedding and, for our honeymoon, went camping in Minnesota's Boundary Waters Canoe Area. We journeyed west in a Toyota Land Cruiser with a pet cat named Misty and a future to be found. But somewhere along the way we'd lost each other.

We were divorced in the spring of 1975. Despondent, I quit work at the forestry college and retreated to the depths of Idaho's Selway Bitterroot Wilderness Area. I spent most of the summer alone with all my worldly possessions stuffed in a Kelty backpack. I read books, climbed mountain peaks, and screamed into the night for something to take the hurt away. I adjusted to being alone, but not to the feeling of loneliness. I longed for some sort of renewed human connection.

And then one day in late August, I decided it was time to do something about my sorry state. I abruptly left the wilderness, returned to civilization, and heard John Denver on the radio. He sang about experiencing a "Rocky Mountain high" and being "born in the summer of his twenty-seventh year."

That's right. I was twenty-seven. And it was the season of new beginnings.

I applied for my first reporter job at the *Daily Idahonian* in Moscow. For some reason, Managing Editor Ted Stanton, who came west from the mighty *Wall Street Journal* to finish a career in newspapering, hired me. It might have had something to do with my willingness to work cheap—for sixty-five dollars a week.

Ted had a mentor's habit of scribbling the words "Good story" across the top of a reporter's work when such kudos were deserved. He also encouraged his staff to look for stories that went beyond the obvious, and he corrected spelling errors without laughing. I lived for his praise.

Reporters like Kenton Bird, Loris Jones, and Wendy Taylor were the soul of the newspaper. They knew how to cover their beats, grind down their sources, and turn in copy on deadline. I think they could have held their own on any so-called big-time newspaper.

But for me, the *Idahonian* became an exercise in on-the-job training. I honed my still meager typing skills, struggled with the pressure of producing daily product, and gradually realized that if I were going to stay in the newspaper business I needed to find a more comfortable niche.

So I began searching. When time allowed, I'd drive into the rolling farm and timber country around Moscow or down into the river canyons to visit towns like Potlatch, Palouse, Uniontown, Kendrick, Juliaetta, Deary, Harvard, and Bovill. As a "general assignment" reporter, I covered city council meetings and small-town gatherings. But I soon sensed that reporting on such events didn't do justice to the communities or the people who lived in them.

Perhaps that's why my trip to Cavendish and visit with Leo Koch became so pivotal. His words struck at the essence of whatever I was becoming as a journalist. They still ring in my head.

"Cavendish used to have a lot more umph. Now it's not even listed in the phone book."

Of course. The phone book!

You could probably flip open to any page, scroll down a column of names, pick a number at random, and find a good story.

I pitched the concept to my editor. But for all his skills that set him apart as an editor and mentor, Ted, like most managing editors, was a pragmatist.

"There's potential, but I think there are already too many other stories out there that we need to do."

He was right. In the media world, small-town dailies are the sweatshops of the industry. The work is never done. Too many stories beg to be told and too few people are around to write them. So I spiked the phone book idea and carried on with the rigors of covering government meetings, the police blotter, and the more obvious feature stories.

I also did my share of obituaries. I found that writing about death was both a righteous and a daunting task. It demanded close attention to detail and a sense of empathy, not so much for the deceased, but for the people we listed as "survivors." If nothing else, "taking obits" over the phone kept reporting in proper perspective. And on one particular day, the job offered me a new life.

— • —

In late June of 1977, one obituary struck me as being particularly tragic because of the victim's young family. Stanley Voss, a twenty-four-year-old carpenter and army veteran from nearby Princeton, had died while horseback riding with his wife. "Voss died Tuesday at Sacred Heart Hospital in Spokane from injuries sustained after a horse threw and kicked him Monday night near Potlatch," I wrote in the obituary. "Survivors include his wife and a nine-month-old daughter."

Some two months later, while researching a story about childbirthing, I was referred by a lay midwife working out of Moscow to her first client: Diane Voss.

Mrs. Voss agreed hesitantly when I called and asked for an interview. She lived at the base of Gold Hill, about three miles north of Princeton, Idaho. I arrived on one of those flaxen warm harvest days when the wheat and barley fields bulge with the season's bounty. After a wrong turn and a run-in with the neighbor's Dobermans, I eased my way up and around to where the world opened up onto a panoramic view of Moscow Mountain and the Palouse farming country. I expected Julie Andrews herself to come bursting over the horizon singing about the hills being alive with the sound of music.

I wasn't even out of the driver's seat when I caught a glimpse of Diane opening the door of the old farmhouse. She was tall, lithe, and tanned, and wore jeans and a T-shirt. Her long blond hair was neatly gathered in a bun atop her head.

"Nice to meet you," she said, holding out her hand to shake mine. She invited me into the living room, where her fox terrier sniffed my ankles and panted with excitement.

"Her name is Missy," said Diane, "Missy boo dog." As I told Diane about the neighbor's Dobermans, a little person with blond hair like her mother's tottered in from around the kitchen corner and interrupted my story.

"And this is Heidi," said Diane, swooping her daughter up into her arms. It wasn't until Heidi returned to the floor and managed to tumble into my camera bag that the coincidence dawned on me. I fumbled for words as I told Diane the odd truth: that I'd written her husband's obituary two months before.

"Oh, yes, I . . . I kept the clipping," said Diane. "Someday I'll show it to Heidi."

Diane launched into her story with a candor that surprised and humbled.

"Stan was first to hold Heidi and cut the umbilical cord," she said, "and we were a family and then . . . it happened so fast. It was a freak accident. We were riding down a gravel road on a beautiful evening with . . . with the smell of freshly mowed hay and wild syringa in the air.

"The horse, it was young and it spooked . . . fell and rolled on him, stood up, kicked Stan in the head . . . and . . . ran to his parents' house half a mile away. Stan didn't move. He was lying there in the road. . . .

"At first I thought he'd just had the wind knocked out of him. I jumped off my horse. Then I . . . I saw he wasn't breathing. His eyes . . . they were dilated, and a neighbor, Keith Schott, heard me screaming. He came running and tried to help. He did mouth-to-mouth. Keith's wife, Jerry, called the ambulance and Stan's family, his dad and brother, started to arrive. I got in the ambulance with Stan . . . I still remember his dad, Ferd, standing there in the road, watching the ambulance drive away with his son."

I stopped taking notes.

"Stan never regained consciousness and died the next day in the hospital. I just couldn't believe it was over. . . . He'd just celebrated his first Father's Day the day before, after attending his little sister's wedding with all the family . . . and his twenty-fifth birthday was just a week away."

Diane talked haltingly while Heidi poked at the tears on her mommy's face. I snapped some photographs, and

16

against my better judgment I found myself taken by this brave, sad woman.

"If it weren't for Heidi, I don't know how I could handle this," Diane confided. "She gives me a reason to wake up each morning. But sometimes I don't even sleep."

About a week later, I called Diane again to ask if I could drop by with a photograph of her holding Heidi. I had already blown up the picture to poster size and could have mailed it. But I hoped to see her again.

When she said "Yes," my heart surrendered.

For me, her husband's recent death made my deepening affection feel somehow wrong. But with each visit to the farm, my feelings intensified. I especially remember the evening we had our first meal together. We dug little red potatoes, pulled carrots and onions, and picked lettuce and tomatoes from the garden to make a late summer stew and salad. I'd never worked so directly for a meal. Afterward, Diane told me about a black bear that came at night and ate plums and apples from trees in the backyard.

Sometimes Diane would take Heidi to Grandma Clara's a couple of miles down the road and we'd saddle the horses to go riding in the woods and hay fields. At first I thought it odd that she'd want even to be near a horse after her husband's death. But when I watched her ride, so upright, confident, and at one with the horse, I knew she'd already struggled through that problem.

"People don't stop driving cars when someone has an accident," she reasoned. "I've always loved horses and riding, and that hasn't changed."

Diane would tell me later that my visits were cathartic at first. I lent an unconditional ear to all that was welling up inside her. And like all moms, she craved conversation with someone other than a one-year-old child. Stan's death, she said, left her feeling like half a person. Somewhere along the line, I started helping her feel whole again. Eventually, whatever it is that brings two people together couldn't be denied.

The first time we hugged good-bye, I felt like a first-grader with no idea of how to get the job done properly. It was kind of a blushing, sideways attempt followed by both of us saying "See ya." I proposed in the spring of 1978 and promised always to keep "Daddy Stan" alive in his daughter's heart.

Diane and Heidi accepted.

— • —

About two months prior to our mid-July wedding, another proposal came my way.

"Hey Johnson, that was a good story you did the other day about zoning. Damn good reporting," the caller barked into the phone. It was Jay Shelledy, executive editor and ringleader of the competing *Lewiston Morning Tribune*.

A week later, Diane and I were sitting at a dinner table in downtown Lewiston, Idaho, with Shelledy and *Tribune* night editor Perry Swisher. While Swisher prefaced his pitch with a lot of questions about whether it would work, Shelledy inhaled a pepper steak and spit out his plan.

"We'd like you to be our rover," he said, explaining that the *Tribune* wanted to put me in a company car and send me into the backcountry with orders never to return without good stories. In other words, they were assigning me to cover everything beyond a fifty-mile radius of Lewiston that had absolutely no news value.

I *loved* the idea.

I resigned from the *Daily Idahonian* in June of 1978, and Diane and I were married a month later in front of the original homestead cabin on land we'd just bought. Heidi, a couple of months short of two years old, held a little basket of wildflowers while the minister led all three of us through the vows. The Voss family, still mourning the death of Stanley, not only attended the wedding, but also gathered me that day into their circle of unconditional love.

I approached Stan's mother, Clara, as she stood alone during the reception.

"I know this is both a happy and sad day for you."

"Yes, it is," she said, smiling. "But I think you're a good man, David. And you better promise to take care of Diane and Heidi."

"I promise."

Diane and I had each other and Heidi, a mortgage on new land, and plans to build a log house atop a hill. I also had a new job that expanded my beat. I ventured eagerly into the depths of the *Lewiston Morning Tribune*'s circulation area—the central Idaho mountains and a sliver of southeastern Washington's Palouse Country. I roamed the two states, visiting such towns as Pierce, Headquarters, Grangeville, Asotin, Kamiah, Kooskia, Pomeroy, Orofino, Dusty, Cottonwood, White Bird, Riggins, and Craigmont. En route, I twisted the car along canyon highways, feasted my eyes on rugged mountains, topped plateaus blanketed in farm fields, and explored forests thick with mystery.

I figured it was the best beat a reporter could have. I also had a hunch that the *Tribune* could become a vehicle for the simple idea that wouldn't stop percolating in the back of my mind. Each foray into hard news convinced me that the phone book offered a microcosmic lens through which I could find the real America.

After our second daughter was born in October of 1980, we realized we'd never leave our home on the hill, and I'd never leave the *Tribune* for another newspaper. Greta joined Heidi in growing up with a dad who drove away a lot and, when he came home, spent too much time on the telephone and typewriter. But even the kids enjoyed the stories I told—not just the ones that appeared in the newspaper, but about the everyday people I met during my travels.

All the more reason why the phone book idea wouldn't go away. I bounced the concept off colleagues now and then. Most predicted that such a column would be too pedestrian. Even Tommy Campbell, a reporting legend at the *Tribune* who was a master at bringing local characters to life on the printed page, politely held his nose.

Diane, in fact, seemed to be my idea's only champion. That is, until the quintessential roving reporter happened to show up on my beat.

— • —

In late 1983, Charles Kuralt of CBS Television's *On the Road* fame came to Washington State University at Pullman, Washington, to speak at the annual Edward R. Murrow Symposium.

I loved watching Kuralt on television and considered him a kindred spirit. He roamed the country in his Winnebago motor home. I cruised the sticks in my Subaru station wagon. Mostly, I liked that he unabashedly skirted the real news to do stories about musical saw players, ice sculptors, and tinkerers who made cars run on corncobs.

I met Kuralt for the first time at a pre-symposium cocktail hour. Scores of local journalists and students attended. Kuralt milled through the crowd with a small entourage of professors and editor types hanging on every folksy word he spoke. Jay Shelledy, never at a loss for words himself, introduced us.

"Charles Kuralt, this is David Johnson, the Charles Kuralt of the *Lewiston Morning Tribune*."

I rolled my eyes and shook Kuralt's hand as Shelledy grinned and upped the ante.

"David Johnson, this is Charles Kuralt, the David Johnson of CBS Television."

Kuralt laughed with that hearty voice that resonated so eloquently over the airwaves. And for some reason, he took great interest in my work. I think it had something to do with a confession he was about to make.

"I was a real reporter once, but I wasn't suited for it by physique or temperament," Kuralt would write about one year later in his first best-seller. "Real reporters have to stick their noses in where they're not wanted, ask embarrassing questions, dodge bullets, contend with deadlines, and worry about competition."

I'd done all of those things, including almost dodging bullets. And like Kuralt, I hadn't really relished any of it. But I liked the feel of a steering wheel in my hands and the search for people who were willing to tell their stories.

Before his remarks Kuralt and I chatted, with drinks in hand, about all the interesting people we'd met and he conceded that "dumb luck" had steered him to some of his best stories. The confession bolstered my confidence and pretty soon I just blurted it out.

"You know, I think a guy could go to the phone book, pick a number randomly, and do a story on whoever answers."

Kuralt, a man of fatherly round proportions, flinched as if somebody had tugged on the back of his rumpled sport coat. "You know," he said, ice tinkling in his glass, "I think that's one of the best ideas I've heard in a long time."

I took a gulp of my drink and caught the approving nod of Jim Godbold, the *Tribune*'s city editor. Godbold, who years later would become executive editor of the *Eugene Register Guard* in Eugene, Oregon, had a flair for feature writing and an appreciation for offbeat ideas. On the strength of Kuralt's endorsement, the two of us went to *Tribune* managing editor Paul Emerson, who'd also heard Kuralt's encouragement.

A stay-the-course kind of guy, Paul listened to my plan, leaned back slightly in his chair, and sighed. "Well," he began slowly, "I think we better make sure it's going to work. Let's see if we can get at least four people, do the interviews, and write the stories."

I drove home that night through the rolling Palouse hills with KGO Radio out of San Francisco issuing traffic reports. There wasn't a car in sight and I laid on the horn to celebrate. I thought of Leo Koch back in his Cavendish Store and the unwitting role he'd played in what was about to happen. Finally, some eight years after getting the phone book idea, I was going to have a chance to prove it worked.

But what if it didn't?

After midnight I quietly crept upstairs, checked the girls to make sure they were tucked in, and found Diane warm in our bed. I hugged her close and whispered, "Guess what? They're going to let me do the column. I'm scared to death."

— • —

The *Lewiston Tribune* was founded in 1892 by two brothers, Eugene L. and Albert H. Alford, when Main Street in Lewiston, Idaho, was dusty in the summer, muddy in the winter, and filled with horse-drawn carriages year round.

As the story goes, the Alfords, both from Texas, took a roundabout route through Oregon to end up in Idaho. They cornered a printing-machinery dealer in Portland

and one of them asked, "Where's a good place to start a newspaper?"

The dealer pointed to the return route of the 1805 Lewis and Clark Expedition and said, "Up the Columbia River and on up the Snake is the little town of Lewiston, Idaho. They're going to open up the Nez Perce Indian Reservation there and the railroad is going in. It looks like a big chance for someone."

The brothers hopped a river steamer and reportedly stepped off in Lewiston, at the confluence of the Snake and Clearwater Rivers, with little more than a "shirttail full of type."

The town had a population of less than a thousand with mostly wooden buildings and just six structures made of brick or stone. More important, and much to the brothers' chagrin, the *Lewiston Teller*, the victor among half a dozen newspapers that had already waged a war for readers, was firmly entrenched in the community.

Despite the odds against making a go of it, the Alfords borrowed money, bought a secondhand press, rented a room in an opera house, and turned out the first edition of the weekly *Lewiston Tribune* on September 29, 1892. Three years later, the *Tribune* became a twice-weekly publication. When the Spanish-American War ignited a demand in 1898 for more news, the paper graduated to an afternoon daily. Less than a year later, it moved to a morning daily, and by October of 1937, it became and has remained the only daily in the Lewiston-Clarkston Valley.

The *Lewiston Morning Tribune*, I'm convinced after more than two decades on the payroll, has remained steeped in the principles of First Amendment journalism because the Alford family wanted it that way.

"Our opinions are not for sale," reads the caption under

an old photograph of late Publisher A. L. (Bud) Alford, Eugene's son.

My favorite *Tribune* sign is posted on the door that opens into the cavernous pressroom, where people with ink-stained hands work amid the roar of tomorrow's news.

Beyond this door, the sign reads, *lies the most powerful freedom weapon in the world. Handle with responsibility.*

With a circulation today of about 30,000, the *Tribune* has been called a "liberal rag" waving in Idaho's conservative political winds. The nineties were tough. Economic forces threatened both the ownership and the future of the *Tribune*. Suffice it to say that the *Lewiston Morning Tribune* remains independently owned by A. L. (Butch) Alford, Jr., and, by virtue of that alone, has become a rarity in contemporary American newspapering.

I prefer to call the *Trib* a noisy little newspaper that pulls no punches and champions fairness as its cornerstone. It's also known as a reporter's newspaper—a daily that encourages individuality among its staff. Management has never, for example, clipped my somewhat flighty journalistic wings.

During my first five years at the *Tribune*, I sometimes spent a tank of gasoline and a ten-hour day scouring the little communities of my backcountry beat before coming up with no "real" news. The frustration fueled my fancy that the phone book might be a hedge against all those dry runs. In theory, the directory could become a more important tool than a pen, notepad, camera, car, or word processor. Because even in a remote place like the Lewiston area, I thought, there were more names in the local telephone book than any reporter could write about in a lifetime. Talk about job security.

Of course, compared to the behemoth directories in America's larger cities, the phone book for north central

Idaho and southeastern Washington is quite humble. Even though it covers eight counties and more than forty towns, it's less than one inch thick.

So it was that in early December of 1983, just weeks after Charles Kuralt had served as unintentional catalyst to launching "Everyone Has a Story," I slipped furtively into the newsroom one evening. Most of the other reporters were taking a dinner break.

In the headlines at the time were stories about U.S. warplanes making retaliatory strikes against Syrian anti-aircraft positions in Lebanon. Polish Solidarity leader Lech Walesa had been awarded the Nobel Prize. And West Germans were expressing shock over *The Day After*, an American-made movie about a nuclear war triggered in Germany.

On the local scene, sinister brothers Mark and Bryan Lankford had pleaded "not guilty" to first-degree murder charges in the bludgeoning deaths of a young marine and his wife in a U.S. Forest Service campground near Grangeville, Idaho.

Against a backdrop of these kinds of "big" stories, I snatched up a phone book and took pains to make sure no witnesses could see or hear what I was about to do. I suspect that inventors feel the same way when testing a new gadget.

After all, I was still wrestling with my stature among the reporters working in the *Tribune* newsroom. It was a seasoned, hard-news staff. And even though I'd spent some five years as the only roving reporter the *Tribune* ever had, I figured there were more dues to pay. In addition to being a bad speller, I'd earned the accurate reputation of leaning toward "human interest" stories rather than mixing it up with politicians and other scoundrels. I knew I wouldn't up my rank if this wacky phone book idea failed.

––––––––

So I huddled at a desk, took a last look around, flipped open the directory, let my fingers do the walking, and opened my eyes.

Marciano Prado.

The name sat there at the tip of my index finger. I looked around again, took a breath, grabbed the phone, and dialed his number. Marciano lived in Kamiah, a town some sixty miles up the Clearwater River from Lewiston on the Nez Perce Indian Reservation.

One of my favorite Nez Perce stories bounced into my head as I listened to the phone ring. According to legend, Coyote had a final fight with the Monster long ago and won. Coyote then ripped the Monster apart, scattering its pieces across the Pacific Northwest. Wherever a piece landed, an Indian tribe was born. The heart of the Monster landed at Kamiah, giving rise to the Nez Perce people.

"Hello," came a young man's voice.

Ruben, the eldest Prado son, had answered. Marciano was at work.

"Well," I said, grasping for words, "maybe *you* can help me." Then I stumbled through my reason for calling, explaining that the *Tribune* was trying this new column about everyday people and . . .

"I think my dad would talk to you," said Ruben.

"He would?" A grin spread across my face.

Exactly one hour later, I was on the phone with Marciano, still hoping no one in the newsroom could hear me talking. Speaking in a heavy Spanish accent, Marciano agreed to talk the next night at his home.

"Damn," I muttered under my breath after hanging up. "It worked."

I looked around. Aside from a copy editor at a distant desk, there was no one else in the newsroom. Part of me wanted to shout "It worked. Hey everybody, it really worked!" But I realized the ultimate test was still ahead.

Would this guy, Marciano Prado, whoever he was, really have a story worthy of space in the *Lewiston Morning Tribune?*

— • —

The road to Kamiah (U.S. Highway 12) is known as Idaho's Killer Highway. Twisting like a black snake into the night along the south edge of the Clearwater River canyon, it offers little escape from head-on traffic. On one side, the river is ready to swallow hapless vehicles that careen from the blacktop. On the other, the steep canyon wall will toss motorists seeking refuge back into harm's way. If that's not enough, the mountains have a nasty habit of sacrificing boulders to gravity's pull. State troopers call accidents on Highway 12 "grinders."

But the roadway can also be a tranquil route along a peaceful river corridor highlighted with historical turnouts like the one near Kamiah called Long Camp. Lewis and Clark's Corps of Discovery bivouacked at the site for a month during the late spring of 1806 on their return trip to St. Louis.

I've logged more than half a million miles on the maze of federal, state, county, and local roads that chisel their way through the *Tribune*'s circulation area. Highway 12 is my favorite because it bisects a region where geography has combined with topography to keep most of civilization's sprawl in check.

Idaho is arguably America's last frontier. More than two-thirds of the state is in national forests and range lands that contain the largest amount of federally classified wilderness acres in the lower forty-eight states. Highway 12 also skirts the southeastern edge of Washington and some of the richest farmland in the country, where truly amber waves of grain stretch between horizons each harvest season.

I never tire of driving these roads. But on this night, my attention reached out beyond the car's headlights to the interview ahead. I really didn't know what to ask. There was no news peg. I was going into an interview as blind and dark as the road ahead.

It took a little over one hour to make the trip, cajoling the wheel and nursing the accelerator through turn after turn. I drove east along the spine of the snake, passing places with names like Spalding, Arrow, Myrtle, Cherry Lane, Agatha, Lenore, and Peck, through the town of Orofino, across the river from the lights of Greer glimmering in the water, over Sixmile Creek, and finally into Kamiah. Nez Perce Chief Lawyer is buried just outside of Kamiah, across the highway from the Heart of the Monster historic site.

Marciano Prado's house, according to young Ruben's directions, was on the near end of town. I confess to having had visions of a stereotype Mexican shack surrounded by pickup trucks, cars, motorcycles, and bikes.

If there's one thing this part of America lacks, it's ethnic diversity. Northern Idaho is a region pretty much filled with people of European ancestry dating back to the arrival of gold miners, loggers, and white homesteaders in the middle to late 1800s. There is, of course, a strong Native American presence with headquarters for the Nez Perce Tribe centrally located in the town of Lapwai. Itinerant Hispanic laborers sometimes come to the area because there is hard work to be done and they aren't afraid of doing it. Marciano, I was soon to find out, came for much more than work.

And so, there was some irony in the fact that the first

random sweep down a page in the telephone book rendered such an atypical subject. Then again, I reflected, the point of the column is that *everyone* has a story.

My headlights swept the house as I turned into Marciano's driveway. I turned off the ignition, stepped out into the black night, heard nervous laughter from inside, and knocked. A young girl opened the door and I introduced myself.

"My dad's in the kitchen," she said, blushing. "Come in."

Marciano came toward me with his hand out, as if I was a long-lost relative. He wore a sweatshirt and sported a mustache that looked like a woolly caterpillar, gaudy plumage that accented Marciano's smile. His hairline was receding and his hands carried the pesky unhealed wounds of someone who labored hard and long.

"Here, come sit down, please," said Marciano, shaking my hand and ushering me to a chair at the kitchen counter. We sat across from each other, me with my notebook and pen, Marciano with his family and story.

"This country, ah, it . . . opens," said Marciano as if he had primed himself for the interview, but was immediately hindered by a lack of language. He struggled for the English words, finally reverting to Spanish and asking Ruben for some help with the translation.

"He said this country received him with arms open. You see, his kids have better opportunities here."

Marciano, father to seven children, nodded his approval.

"People say, 'Why did you come to the United States?'" said Marciano, pausing to shake his head. The answer was obvious. "To support my family."

Born and raised in Tocatzeuaro, Mexico, to Jesus and Eloisa Prado, Marciano said he hadn't forgotten where he came from. Neither had his wife, Bertha, nor the Prado children, who ranged in age from ten to nineteen. The family photo album traced the years back to when times were not so good. He showed me a picture of fourteen-year-old Martha as a child, sitting alone in what the Prados described as a "one-room cardboard shack"—their home in Mexico.

I expressed my admiration for their small, well-kept home, pleasing Bertha and making private amends for my earlier biased thoughts. There was a utilitarian feel to the way the living and dining rooms shared space and a single hallway led to the bedrooms and bath. The family was proud of what they had. Nothing had been given to them. Marciano had worked for twelve years as a cedar maker at the local mill, rendering huge trees into roofing shakes, fence posts, and rails. The hard work required hour upon hour of driving steel wedges with heavy mauls in the heat of summer and the cold of winter.

"Really, I surprise myself because I don't know how we make it," Marciano confided.

While her husband and I talked, Bertha busied herself at the stove. She had delayed dinner. Five of the Prado children, Ruben, nineteen; Delia, fifteen; Martha, fourteen; Marciano, Jr., thirteen; and Daniel, ten, crowded around us. Albert, eighteen, and Israel, seventeen, weren't home.

"I've got a sister who has sixteen children," Marciano announced, as if the number of offspring were a relative matter.

Back around 1970, Marciano said, his mother, Eloisa Hamilton (who'd earlier moved to Kooskia, Idaho), suggested that he and his family move to the area from California. The advice was good, Marciano and Bertha agreed.

"There is much reason to be thankful," Bertha said, turning from the stove to join the periphery of the conversation.

Marciano worked as a gyppo (a term used in logging circles to mean he got paid for how much he produced). The gyppos at the Star Cedar Mill, he explained, had a system by which they shared one another's profits. Some days were good, others not so good.

"Today I didn't even make half of my wages," Marciano said. Sometimes, he lamented, it would be better to work for an hourly wage. But in the long run, getting paid for what you produce is better for everyone, he said.

I thought about my own job and salary. Here I was, arriving by chance in the kitchen of a total stranger on the premise that my employer would pay me for the effort, even if the story didn't pan out. I hadn't considered it before, but there is a certain amount of luxury in knowing you'll get paid regardless of the outcome.

"It was difficult for me when I come up here and go to work at the mill," said Marciano. "But I learn quick. One day, I even made one hundred dollars."

Marciano and I were soon exchanging financial woes as I told him about the twenty-five years to go on my mortgage.

"We just keep paying too," Marciano agreed.

Then our conversation moved on to happier things, like what the children were doing.

Marciano nodded at my description of Heidi, seven, and Greta, three. With at least three of his younger kids hanging on his shoulders at all times, he listed their accomplishments. Ruben, who looked forward to college, was a heavyweight wrestler for the Kamiah High School Kubs. Israel also wrestled on the team. Martha was a cheerleader. Delia liked track and was a whiz on the typewriter. "Junior" wrestled in the seventh grade. And Daniel, a fourth-grader, had yet to think of a career. I asked him if he planned to be a wrestler too.

He nodded yes and hid behind his dad.

By this time, I found myself doing more talking than interviewing. I had no idea how to write Marciano's story, but I knew it was there. Why else would I be so interested?

Meanwhile, the aroma of Bertha's cooking got the best of me.

"Dinner," said Marciano. Every day, he explained, he ate Bertha's chili, refried beans, and tortillas. The menu usually included something else, but the three staples were always served. The children, at least the older ones, liked Mexican dishes now and then. Martha preferred pizza and an Idaho mainstay, "spuds."

But at forty-six, Marciano reasoned, his tastes went back to childhood in Mexico and his appetite was set in its ways.

"This one is not too hot," he said, pulling a bottle of salsa from the cupboard.

"Would you like some chili?"

I practically drooled in response to the steaming bowl.

Bertha, anticipating Marciano's invitation for another mouth at the table, had a bowl ready and filled it up. The children giggled and gathered around to watch. "It's really hot," warned Delia. "Watch out!"

Ruben was on his way to the water faucet as I shoveled the first spoonful into my mouth. By the time my eyes started watering and my tongue had retreated into my larynx, the glass was in front of me and I doused the fire while everyone laughed at the same old joke played on a new victim.

I nursed the rest of my chili, realizing I'd need more time to adapt to real Mexican food. Marciano, turning to Ruben again for help with the language, summed up the difference between Mexico and the United States.

"That's our home country. But this country is our home."

As if to punctuate the thought, he took a heaping spoonful of chili, looked me straight in the eye, and swallowed.

———

He didn't even flinch.

On January 6, 1984, the day Marciano's story ran as the first of what would become hundreds of "Everyone" columns, a headline on the *Tribune*'s front page read: "Poor results blamed on weak family unit." The story was about how a nationwide drop on college test scores and a rise in high school dropouts were reflections of the troubled state of American families.

As families go, the Prados were indeed of the old-fashioned, nuclear variety. It was a patriarchy by tradition and perhaps necessity. Marciano's children not only swarmed around him at the dinner table, but the quality of their young lives revolved around his ability to work with his hands and, teamed with Bertha, to make a home. I'd quite literally tasted the warmth of this family. I wanted to hug them all, or pay them, or do something to express my gratitude. They'd shared their story so openly and gotten "Everyone" off to a running start.

Some five years later, on August 5, 1989, the *Lewiston Morning Tribune* went to press as usual and around daybreak arrived on the doorsteps of homes throughout north central Idaho and southeastern Washington. There were front-page headlines about a sex scandal in Washington, D.C., possible release of American hostages in Beirut, and the eighty-ninth birthday bash for Britain's Queen Mother Elizabeth.

About the same time, at 5:05 A.M. near Kamiah on that same killer highway I'd driven that dark night in late 1983 to meet the Prado family, Marciano was walking alone. He'd been drinking. In the opposite direction, another Kamiah man was driving his 1972 Ford pickup truck.

The next day's story still haunts me. I read it after jogging down our half-mile-long driveway to the Hatter Creek Road and snatching my *Trib* from the yellow box propped on a metal fence post. Buried at the bottom of the obituary page were the words: "Kamiah resident Marciano M. Prado, 51, was struck early Saturday morning in an accident with a passing motorist. Prado, who was walking in the west lane of traffic before being hit, was killed instantly."

I called Bertha and we cried on the phone together.

CHAPTER TWO

Creating a Home

Before the column, before we'd met, even before Stan and Heidi, Diane had begun designing her dream home—sketched on a piece of paper at age eight by a little girl who wanted nothing more than an old-fashioned homestead constructed of Lincoln Logs and love. So when in April 1978, a few months shy of our wedding, she heard about the land, she called me immediately.

"Do you have time? We could drive up there and look at it right now."

"How much land are we talking about here?"

"I think it's about a hundred and twenty acres; I'm not sure. But it's for sale and nobody else knows about it."

The excitement in Diane's voice was undeniable. We were engaged to be married and had been looking for some property in the country. My mind was almost set on a place near Deary where a number of friends had already become contemporary homesteaders. I took comfort in knowing that a few familiar pioneers had already broken ground and could lend me their expertise about country living.

But Diane seemed bent on adventure and the romance of finding our own special place in the woods.

"This is kind of steep," I said after we parked the car along the county road and began trekking up the remnants of an old driveway onto this secret piece of real estate. Part of the approach was washed out and small trees stood as impediments to any vehicular traffic.

"Oh, come on," said Diane. She took my hand and we walked in perfect unison. To this day, we still walk that way. It's got something to do with similar inseams. Our strides match exactly; at least when we agree on destinations. And to tell the truth, we weren't exactly in sync this time. I wasn't so sure about where she was taking me.

"How would we plow our way out of here in the winter?" I asked as my breath grew heavier.

"With a plow."

"And water. Where the heck are we going to find water?" I said, stopping to debate the practicality of such a remote location.

"In a well," said Diane, continuing to move ahead. "We'll drill a well."

It was that simple for her. Where there's a will, there's a well. And I could tell that with each uphill step taken, the woman with whom I wanted to spend the rest of my life was climbing toward a personal paradise.

"Oh look," she all but shouted. "Isn't it beautiful? It's so beautiful."

We'd rounded the first turn on this sorry excuse for a driveway and had come out into the open.

"What a view. Look at the view!" By now, Diane had shucked my hand aside and increased her pace up the hill and around the next turn. I'm pretty sure her feet left the ground and she floated most of the way up the hill.

"Oh, look at the cabin, David. Look at the cabin!"

At the top of what turned out to be a half-mile-long horseshoe-shaped driveway stood a one-room log building. We'd later learn that a resourceful man named Alec Bull built the cabin and lived there with his family during the Great Depression. Weathered gray against the blue sky of early April, the cabin clung to life under a roof of tattered cedar shakes.

I pushed again and again on a door so resistant I'd have sworn it was pushing back against *me*. Then, with one well-placed thrust of my right leg, I kicked open the door. Daylight rushed inside and the darkness disappeared. The entrance opened into what my daughters would call the "olden days." Diane and I poked around, touched the walls, pretended to warm our hands over the slumping brick fireplace, and talked about what it must have been like to live in such a house.

"Where the heck did they get their water?" I asked again.

Diane didn't seem to care. She was already building her own log home in her mind. I can still see the excitement in her eyes and the way the amber-colored light betrayed her thoughts. Nothing, even dehydration, would deny such determination.

Beyond the old cabin, the hill leveled off onto a flat ridge. Grass, waving in the wind, covered most of the ground and had undoubtedly been cut for hay each year. The forest, with trees reaching high against the horizon, provided a buffer from winter winds to the north and consumed the rest of the property for half a mile to the west.

"We could build right here," said Diane as we reached the highest place on the property. "The house would face straight south, to get the sun, especially in the winter. I love sun," said Diane. "I love this place. Don't you? How could you not?"

Diane has never been one to get down on her knees and

beg for anything. But she knows about taking advantage of opportunity when it's at hand. And so did I.

Beckoning to her, I took off my coat and placed it on a mat of grass.

"Right here?" she asked.

I didn't answer. She smiled as I leaned her backward in my arms—like in one of those old-fashioned movies starring Fred Astaire and Ginger Rogers. I cupped Diane's face in my hands and we touched noses.

"Where the heck are we going to find water?" I whispered. Diane answered with a little shrug of her shoulders and a long kiss.

Lying there in Diane's arms, I listened to the wind drifting through the long grass and warmed to the thought of a log home on a hill. Mostly, though, I felt Diane's desire for me and the ground beneath us.

— • —

Before meeting Diane, I'd long fancied living at the rural end of civilization's spectrum, maybe even off the grid. Alaska seemed like a good option. But I came to Idaho and found the wilderness not all that far away. And sometimes I'd dream about the adventures of men like Jim Renshaw.

Most people live in cities. Others take to the country. A few exceptional people live so close to the land that they become part of it. I thought I might be that way, but my "Everyone" interview with Jim Renshaw helped set me straight.

If an election were held to pick someone who epitomized Idaho's frontier mystique, Jim would have been the true-grit candidate. He chose to live as far away from cities as he could. His phone rang in his house a short way up Suttler Creek. But his soul traversed the deeper recesses of Idaho's backcountry. And the way I saw it, Jim's arrival in the world was about a century late.

"I think if I'd lived back in the eighteen hundreds," he said, "I could have been a mountain man."

Jim wore a Stetson on his head, a big buckle on his belt, a cowboy shirt, denim jeans, and boots made for riding, not walking. The garb was pure utility, not fashion. He loved pack animals and when he hugged a mule, they both seemed to smile. By contemporary measures, he was indeed a mountain man. Born in the lusty logging town of Kooskia, Idaho, he moved with his parents to the Selway River country as an infant.

"They took me to the mountains when I was two months old. I've been pretty close to 'em ever since." He was raised in the midst of millions of acres now classified by federal law as the Selway Bitterroot Wilderness Area.

"I always figured the black sheep went to the Selway," Jim said.

I was the Selway black sheep of my family. I left my childhood home in Minnesota and had no plans to return. During the summer of 1975, when I was mending from my divorce, I chose to be homeless and flounder around in the Selway country. Aside from the contemporary comforts of a down sleeping bag, a waterproof tarp, and freeze-dried food, I lived a wonderfully austere life. Every night I lit a campfire, cooked some freeze-dried food, and slept on the ground. Some of my city friends still can't fathom why it was good for me to do that. But Jim Renshaw understood.

"That country can clean your mind up."

Maybe even your heart, I thought.

A hearty fifty-four years old when I met him, Jim had been working as an outfitter and hunting guide for more than three decades. He preferred coaxing mules out of the mountains to piloting a Cadillac down a freeway.

———

"It's a prestige thing . . . to have a good string of mules behind me." The animals, he said, were like a good woman—hard to come by and worth their weight in gold.

I thought of Diane. She'd probably like the comparison.

"I like my mules and they like me," said Jim. "You hear people say that you have to get a mule's attention with a two-by-four. Well, nobody hits my mules." And probably nobody felt more at home in wild country than Jim Renshaw.

"Went to California for a few days. What I remember most is the airplanes landed at Los Angeles about every thirty seconds." Upon his return to Idaho, Jim took a three-day snowshoe trip back into the Selway just to recover from culture shock.

"I like to hunt. I like to pack mules and I like the back-country," said Jim, summing up his passion. "I'm at home where there are no houses, no roads, no people, and no roofs over my head."

Some fifteen years have passed since we talked. But each autumn I go vicariously to the wilderness with Jim, just to stay in touch with that far end of the spectrum. I know now that I'm simply not tough enough to live at that extreme. But I like thinking about Jim out there with his rifle, his mules, and the land he loves all around him. It makes me reflect back to that day in 1978 when I stood not in the middle of the wilderness, but in a place that nonetheless made me feel something wild stirring inside me.

— • —

As far as my eyes could see, no trappings of civilization broke the landscape—except for the steep driveway and old cabin we'd discovered a few days earlier.

"Go back up there by yourself," Diane had urged. "Sit up there and think about it."

When it came to choosing a place to live, I was stubbornly stuck on those practical things men are supposed to fret about, especially in a rural setting—like maintaining the driveway, getting electricity up the hill, and, of course, finding water.

But I took Diane's suggestion and went back by myself to look at the land she already loved. I had a sneaking suspicion, as I walked to the top of the hill in a gentle shower, that she knew the time alone would bring me to her way of thinking.

The rain drifted down from the clouds, caressing the land the way it always does in northern Idaho late in April. Moscow Mountain had shed its winter-white coat to show off a kelly green meadow below, and songbirds flitted around in celebration.

The old cabin stood stalwart at the crest. The building already seemed like a familiar friend. Its windows were gone, the door was still stuck, and the cedar-shake roof seemed to be working overtime to shed the late afternoon shower. I rubbed my hands over the wet, weathered logs and peered through a crack to find the confines dark but still inviting. I wondered again about the people who'd lived long ago in the little cabin.

"Maybe they had a well somewhere out back," I mumbled.

To the south, the clouds began to yawn and the sun shown through ever so slightly. Wisps of steam rose from the forest floor and, as far as my imagination would let me pretend, not a single building or any hint of towns or highways separated me from the land. In fact, only the songbirds chirping and the rain pattering on the old cabin roof broke the afternoon's stillness.

Then a buck exploded from tall grass not ten yards away. I grabbed my breath at its sudden appearance. My loitering had apparently unnerved him. Feeling vulnerable, the deer trotted another ten yards and stopped. His short velvet antlers were bathed in droplets of water. His left side, the one that had been nestled against the ground, was dry and shone amber in the fading light of day.

"Hey there," I said. "Aren't you a handsome fellow."

My heart, like his, no doubt, pounded with surprise, and we stood there getting acquainted. His eyes locked on mine and mine on his. Then the buck slowly lifted his white tail and walked away, disappearing into the fog that rose from the draw below the cabin. I snatched up a timothy stem, stuck it between my teeth, and chewed around the smile on my face.

"Far out," I mused in the John Denver vernacular of the day.

Then I turned, like the deer, to walk away. I knew at that moment that Diane was right. If we could find the wherewithal, this could be our place. This would be our home— so far and so different from where I grew up.

— • —

Sometimes I wonder why, after being raised in the Minneapolis suburbs, I gravitated west. Maybe my childhood fascination with wagon trains and explorers drove me. Living *on* the land, as Diane wanted so desperately to do, is not the same as living *off* the land. She had no pretensions of us becoming farmers or ranchers. But I knew she dreamed of finding a place to raise a family and maybe leave a mark.

Tom and Vicki Petty helped me grasp that concept when the column brought me to their doorstep. They lived on

Cloverland Ridge about twenty-five miles southwest of Clarkston, Washington. Their four-generation family homestead was located out where the pavement ended and the gravel road began, where about sixteen inches of rain fell each year and wheat went about sixty bushels to the acre.

The Pettys were farmers. But more than that, they were proprietors of the land and keepers of a family legacy.

"It's all been homesteaded at one time or another," said Tom, referring to the fourteen-mile ridge of farming country that dropped off to George Creek on the east and Asotin Creek on the west, and offered a distant view of the Lewiston-Clarkston Valley to the northeast.

The Petty farm, where Tom was raised and had plans to stay, dated back to 1879, when Hubbard Petty, Tom's great-grandfather, settled the land. Two homestead deeds, one signed by President Benjamin Harrison and the other by President Chester A. Arthur, were but two historical documents cherished by the family. A dog-eared Bible listing the birthdays of relatives was yet another heirloom.

I carefully probed the pages of the Bible, marveling at not just the weight of God's word but also at the texture of all those names on the tattered pages. Such a sense of belonging a tome like that must instill.

The Pettys worked some 800 acres, most of it their own, some of it rented from neighbors. About sixty-five people lived on Cloverland Ridge. All but a few were farmers. "I wouldn't say there's any drawbacks to living up here," said Tom—other than the constant battle to make ends meet.

Farmers literally and figuratively cultivate a relationship with the land. They till the soil, bring dirt home on their clothes, fret about crop failures, bemoan poor market prices, reap a bounty when times are good, and raise their children to do the same. They build houses and surround them with outbuildings and eventually invest so much of themselves in what they've created that their home becomes a barometer of where their lives are going. Sooner or later, such farms become known by the last name of the families who live there.

I left the Petty Place on that brisk March day with spring planting just around the corner. Tom said the ground was dry enough to work but cold weather still threatened.

"No need to get excited."

Unless the weather jogged the schedule, the fields would soon turn green with spring's arrival—just like when the first of the Pettys turned over the soil and decided this was a good place to lay down roots and call it home.

I think Diane had borrowed a page from the Pettys' playbook when we first walked up that driveway and reached the top of the hill. She was ready to consummate a new relationship, to commit herself to the proposition of building the Johnson Place from the ground up.

— • —

"I have some money," Diane said hesitantly one day.

"What do you mean?"

"From insurance . . . I wanted to tell you before. . . . I mean, I really did, but I just wanted to make sure you were marrying me for the right reasons."

We'd just finished dinner in the old farmhouse where Diane continued to live after her husband's death. A Paul Anka album played in the background as Heidi slept in her crib. I stared across the table as Diane continued.

"The insurance people, they advised me not to tell anybody for a while."

"Insurance for what?" I asked.

"Stan. There was a life insurance policy, a couple of

them. And I haven't told anyone, except Stan's parents know. I just . . . I wasn't sure. I wanted to make sure the money, you know, that you wanted me, not the—"

"The money. I didn't . . . I don't know anything about any money."

"I know," said Diane. "But there's enough, I think, to buy some land and . . ."

A sudden sense of guilt overwhelmed me. I'd always been uncomfortable having met and fallen in love with Diane so closely on the heels of Stan's death. Now, as this new revelation sank in, I began to wish we'd met maybe a year or more later. My intentions, I feared, could be misjudged—if not by Diane herself, then by people who would assume I was after a widow's bank account. I mean, what else could they think?

"It doesn't make any difference one way or another," I said. "You've got to know that."

"I hope not," said Diane, smiling as if she'd just floated a trial balloon and been pleased to see that, so far, nothing had popped.

"It doesn't," I whispered, reaching across the table for her hand. "It doesn't make any difference. . . . Please believe me." I felt like I was talking not so much to Diane but to everyone else who might hear of the secret.

The money, of course, did make a difference. Dollars can't buy love, but they can finance dreams, or at least provide a good down payment. Most people work nearly a lifetime pursuing flights of fancy like owning "a little piece of heaven." Elsewhere in America, such a place might be a lavish high-rise apartment or condo in the suburbs. In Idaho, everyone seems inclined to live on a hill.

Lyle and Phyllis Walker found their portion of paradise long before Diane and I stumbled onto our pending real estate deal. When I interviewed them for the column they were living in retirement near Kooskia, Idaho, way up on Tahoe Ridge, and they claimed to have it all: seven good children, nine grandchildren, a small herd of cattle, two dogs, some chickens, a television and microwave oven, more springwater than they needed, a good view, a decent retirement income, 128 acres, and a house built to float.

"The man who built it was a preacher," Phyllis told me, "and he was sure a flood was coming. Everyone called him Stud Horse Gil."

Stud Horse Gil?

"He thought himself and twelve women would be the only ones who'd survive," Phyllis explained.

Lyle, who was fifty-six, and Phyllis, fifty-five, didn't worry about things like floods, death, and the hereafter.

"I'd just as soon have my ashes thrown back there in the mountains somewhere," said Lyle, casting a glance over his shoulder.

"I could care less," Phyllis said, shrugging, in answer to the question of where her remains would finally settle. "I don't think I'll know."

Up there on Tahoe Ridge, where the sun rose, shone, and set on the mountains all day long, the Walkers already considered themselves pretty close to heaven. I pondered that old biblical saying about ashes to ashes and dust to dust. In Idaho, I knew from doing other stories, you can actually be buried on your land. Diane knew that too.

"We just love it here," said Lyle. "I've been in thirty-three states and I wouldn't move back to anyplace but right here."

"I really feel that we've got as good a place as any place in the world," Phyllis agreed.

When the Walkers moved in 1970 to what most people now called Walker Canyon, they owned the only mailbox at the top of Tahoe Ridge. But there'd been a population explosion of sorts. I counted five mailboxes down at the corner.

"And if you get in the right spot, you can see someone else's light at night," said Phyllis.

I looked out the window of the Walker home across the valley to Cottonwood Butte on the distant western horizon. Wasn't there *anything* negative about living here?

Lyle and Phyllis looked at each other, shrugged, and agreed that nothing posed a problem, except an occasional rambunctious breeze.

All in all, a small price to pay for a piece of heaven and a dream house built to float.

Diane had retained the drawing of her dream house she'd sketched in the third grade. Set on a hill, the cabin was two stories tall with an attached greenhouse and a porch out front, a dining area with big windows, a master bedroom upstairs, and plenty of space for kids and pets.

"You drew this when you were a kid?" I asked.

"I'm still drawing it in my mind," she answered.

The house, predictably, was made of large logs.

"We had Lincoln Logs when I was a kid," she reflected, "but never enough to build the house I wanted."

One thing I knew for sure. Bachelorhood in any kind of house was not to my liking. I'd been living alone in a small house in Moscow since my divorce in 1975, and despite the bustling nature of my work, I would sometimes be overwhelmed with sadness and fear of spending the rest of my life alone.

I revisited those difficult times many years later while spending a pensive afternoon with Delano Coy, a man who'd loved, lost, and never received another chance.

Delano, of Colfax, Washington, had just moved into a new apartment when I called. He was trying to cut expenses and thereby acquire a new lease on life.

"I'm still struggling," he said of his financial circumstances. "I don't think I could hold down a full-time job anymore."

We sat at the dining table between the tiny kitchen and the unpretentious living room of his new apartment. At fifty-eight, Delano seemed as unassuming as his home, which was sparsely furnished. A couch and a couple of chairs. A kitchen table and a couple more chairs. An end table or two. A lamp here and there.

For an income, Delano received monthly Social Security disability checks and a meager pension from his years as a baker. The money paid the rent, but couldn't reimburse him for the blow he'd suffered fifteen years earlier.

"I had a stroke and was unconscious for about thirty days." When he awoke, Delano realized his life was forever changed. He was relegated to a rest home. He and his second wife were divorced two years later. Eventually he relocated to Colfax, where he moved into an apartment and qualified for an assisted living program.

"There are memories in there, but I can't put them in chronological order," Delano said of his frustration with the past. "I've had a few minor strokes since then."

The father of six grown children by two marriages, Delano said he lived alone by choice. But I wondered about that. Each day, he conceded, offered little more than the previous. So he tried to leaven the monotony with a bit of humor.

"All I do is watch TV and walk the streets and I don't make much money doing it," he quipped.

His meager income had given him a somewhat curious appreciation of Colfax. "We don't have much to do here, but I can't do that much anyway," he said. "So it's a good place for me. There's no frustrating yourself, knowing there's something out there and you can't do it."

Hobbies?

"I wish I had one," said Delano. He played never-ending games of solitaire at the kitchen table to help pass the time. In his mind, he paid fifty-two dollars for a deck of cards and rewarded himself with five dollars for every card he turned over.

"I think I owe myself a million dollars now," he said.

When he needed to get somewhere, he walked. "I'm not driving anymore because I'm afraid I might hit someone." And since he walked so much, he tried to help those who couldn't help themselves.

"I help a lot of the elderly ladies. I run errands for them."

A parishioner at the local Saint Patrick's Church, Delano said he'd long ago come to grips with the future. "I made my peace with God, so I'm all right there. Whatever happens, happens." He was content to live by modest means, watch a little television, play some solitaire, lend a hand to neighbors, and come home each day to his apartment.

"I think I'll like it here."

I drove away thinking again about my three years of bachelorhood prior to meeting Diane. Like most men, I wasn't much of a housekeeper or interior decorator. My home was little more than a building where I could stock the refrigerator, wash the dishes now and then, take a shower, fall asleep with talk radio in my ear, and wake to what tomorrow offered.

"I know how you felt," Diane would later tell me. "When Stan died, I was afraid of being alone for the rest of my life. I hadn't just lost my husband, I felt like I'd lost my family. And I didn't know where Heidi and I were going to live."

Diane and Stan had been renting the house where I met her. The Vosses owned the place. And Diane knew Stan's parents wanted to keep the farmstead in the family. So she was already grappling with the uncertainties of being alone in the world with a toddler at her side.

"I have Heidi and I really don't get out, or go places," she said. "I didn't expect somebody like you to come walking into my life."

Wanting, *needing* a place to call our own, we put a down payment on the acreage and set up a thirty-year mortgage.

About a month later, on July 15, 1978, we got married in front of the old homestead cabin. I mowed a path all the way up the steep driveway in ninety-degree heat and gained a new appreciation for the work ethic of Alec Bull. Neighbors said he built the entire driveway with a wheelbarrow, pick, and shovel.

About forty family members and friends attended the nuptials on a sun-soaked morning that was no less than glorious. A photographer from the newspaper shot the celebration. My favorite picture was taken from inside the old cabin looking out the door as the minister helped us recite our vows. Diane wore a white, full-length muslin dress with delicate flowers embroidered on the yoke and sash. She made the gown for twenty-five dollars and my matching shirt for less. In the picture, our heads are tipped toward each other ever so slightly. I've got my left arm around Diane's waist. And cradled in my right arm, looking back over my shoulder, is Heidi sucking on a bottle of milk.

"We've got to get these things framed and hang them on a wall," I've told Diane scores of times since we were married.

"What wall?" she answers.

Like so many of my good intentions, the display of wedding photographs awaits completion of a special focal point worthy of such priceless memories. I just can't seem to get around to building the wall. For that matter, I'm embarrassed to say that our house, like the Lincoln Log house of Diane's childhood, remains unfinished.

"Someday," I promise.

"Someday," she muses.

— • —

Lowell Davis and Carmen O'Hara offered me some solace shortly after my finger settled on their names in the phone book. They began building their own dream home on a hill about the time Diane and I had hired an attorney to secure the legal link to our land. More than a roof over their heads, Lowell and Carmen wanted to craft a lifestyle and maybe a statement about the times.

"When I started building this house, I guess I was on some kind of a mission to change the world," Lowell said, recalling his earlier back-to-the-land plan.

"If you'd seen the driveway, it was definitely back to the land," Carmen added.

Lowell, who was forty-two, and Carmen, thirty-four, lived high above the Clearwater River. Most people, no matter where they live, gradually become part of a place, and a sense of pride wells up within the walls they erect. Lowell and Carmen shared a palpable satisfaction in their homeplace.

Diane wanted that to happen with us. She already took great pride in designing a house and yearned to put her signature on the finished product, to instill her own sense of decor and utility within the confines of a home. I understood the longing but didn't quite share it.

Lowell and Carmen, on the other hand, were equally committed to a home that mirrored their take on life.

"We've got a few years of work left," Carmen said as I sat down in the kitchen on a wintry day. Already the two-story home stood as a monument to whatever Carmen and Low-ell had become as a couple. If anything tested a relationship, they said, it was building a house that embodied the amalgamation of two independent personalities.

"We started the house before we got married, just in case it didn't work out," said Carmen. Then they drew up a prenuptial agreement, just in case the marriage didn't work.

Like Diane and I, Lowell and Carmen were married on their property, just below the house where a rock outcrop overlooked the Clearwater River breaks far below.

"It was going to be a happy hippie commune," Lowell said, laughing, as he remembered that first land purchase. But once construction began, both he and Carmen swallowed a dose of pride. Going back to the land didn't seem quite as attractive as it had before.

"I finally convinced myself that suffering isn't virtuous," Lowell said. No electricity, no water, no telephone—going without seemed like the avenue to a simpler life. But after living without these staples, Lowell and Carmen came to realize that such amenities pose no intrinsic evil. And with that concession, the home went from a place without electricity and running water to more comfortable surroundings.

Almost ten years later I called Carmen to see if the house had continued to change and, if it had, whether the changes still spoke to their take on life.

"Yes, it has changed," Carmen confirmed. "We added a huge addition . . . the children's wing."

The evolution of house and couple into home and family had taken another decade, but the process appeared to be complete. "We have two beautiful daughters," Carmen reported. Jasmen was five and Maya was three.

The house, instead of a statement about ideals, had become that and more, Carmen explained. It was a place where their children were now secure with a mom and a dad who probably weren't ready to be parents when they first started building.

— • —

Our house logs arrived on the back of a semi-tractor trailer and it took four loads.

"Big house," said Ed Dorman, owner of a company called North Idaho Log Homes. We hired Ed to build because he possessed the skills necessary to turn a pile of logs into a solid structure *and* because he offered a handshake that convinced me he'd get the job done for a reasonable price. I was right.

One by one the huge white-pine logs were lifted into place, just like the eight-year-old had done with those Lincoln Logs. Finally, after about a week, Ed worked the controls of an extended boom to lower the ridgepole carefully into position.

"Done," he announced with a satisfied smile.

I squinted at his work. With a little imagination, I could see Diane's dream. But what Ed left behind was nowhere near a finished house. He and his helpers had notched all the logs together and used a chainsaw to cut openings for windows and doors. The rest was up to us.

"What do you think?" I asked Diane as Ed drove away with most of her insurance money.

"I love it."

To me, the house looked like a huge pile of firewood neatly stacked and ready for a match. But I was determined to finish what had been started. By this time, we were living in a little mobile home about one hundred yards from the house site. We could saunter over and do a little work whenever possible. This, in fact, became our routine for the next year. I continued reporting for the *Tribune* and spent evenings, weekends, and vacations working on the house.

When the time was right, we invited friends out for a roofing party. They did more work in one weekend than Diane and I could have done in two months. With the roof protecting the logs, we pounded down flooring. We sand-blasted the interior walls to bring color back to the weath-ered logs. We stuffed insulation in between the logs and Diane wore out three electric hand sanders trying to make the logs as smooth as possible. We installed windows and built a two-story concrete chimney. We hired an electri-cian and plumber. We built a hearth of stone to hold a woodstove and—I almost forgot. Before all that, we found water.

At the head of the draw below the house, where the deer had disappeared in the fog on that day I visited the prop-erty alone, Ed McPherson drilled a well. He bored two hundred and twenty feet below the earth's surface, and to this day we drink with a special appreciation for the cool, clear water he tapped.

Finally, two days before Christmas in 1982, we hung the front door only moments before my family arrived from Minnesota to spend the holidays.

"Oh David and Diane, it's so beautiful," exclaimed my sister, Maryanne.

"Well, it's far from finished," I hedged.

"Wow, what a place!" another relative marveled in be-tween hugs.

"It's like a giant Lincoln Log cabin!"

I looked at Diane. She was exhausted. So was I. But as house warmings go, the Christmas of 1982 was indeed a benchmark.

Later, Marjorie Deerkop, the subject of another "Everyone" column, helped convince me that building a warm, lasting homestead was well worth the trouble. As we talked on a cloudy October day with a hint of winter around the corner, the furnace in her home kept turning on and off. She'd harvested vegetables from the garden days before. The tamarack trees on Gold Hill were beginning to turn. The timing was good, she said, for opening the cedar chest and unfolding the old quilt.

"They did everything the hard way," said Marjorie, sixty-seven, spreading the blanket on her lap. A good quilt is like an old home, Marjorie explained. You can wrap yourself in its warmth and sentiment.

More than seven decades earlier, on a windswept ranch in Montana, probably during the evening hours when winter piled snow outside the door, Louisa Garey, Marjorie's grandmother, took needle and thread in hand to create a patchwork of memories.

"You see, these have cotton inside," Marjorie said, touching the individual pieces of cloth that had been hand-sewn by her grandmother. "Cotton has a tendency to clump. That's why they quilted so closely. And they used every scrap they could come by."

In the old days, necessity dictated that form always follow function. Quilts, Marjorie said, teamed up with a sturdy home as buffers against winter's crisp nights.

"But they made them for beauty too," she said. Her grandmother's quilt was an example of both art and craft. Though tattered along the edges, its seams remained taut and its design stood as testament to an artistic hand. I felt the quilt's texture and rubbed it against my cheek. Already it had withstood the test of time. Folded back into the cedar chest, it remained ready to be passed to the next generation. Marjorie said she'd probably have her children and grandchildren draw slips of paper to see who'd inherit the quilt.

"That way they won't fight over it," she said, smiling.

A widow of two years, Marjorie lived alone in Princeton, Idaho, not far down the Hatter Creek Road from our home. She tended a large garden, traveled when she could, and every Wednesday ventured to nearby Harvard, where the women of the Ladies Aid did their needlework. The gatherings were a throwback to the old days, when socializing was done in places like Grange halls, churches, community centers, and sometimes the living room of a home. Women met to talk and nourish the bonds of friendship while turning fabric and thread into heirlooms.

"We never make appointments for Wednesday because that's quilting day," Marjorie said.

I couldn't stitch a quilt for Diane. But by building a home that she could wrap around herself and her family, I hoped she could live her dream. In retrospect, I also wanted to build a place where she could guard against a nightmare.

— • —

"My worst fear," Diane said one day while we were working on the house, "is that I'll end up like Mama."

The words didn't seem all that foreboding when she uttered them more than two decades ago. But I think about what she said whenever I drive State Highway 6 along the Palouse River. Out on the flats, away from the highway, rests a little house by two aging fir trees. Diane's mother lived there after separating from her husband.

John and Alice Meschko had four children. Diane was

the oldest of three daughters and a son. By the time Diane and I met, her sisters and brother were grown and living away from home. Daddy, as Diane called her father, had moved to St. Maries and was nearing retirement from the U.S. Forest Service. Mama, as Diane called her mother, had lived alone in the house on the flats since the children left.

As a child, Diane lived in seven different houses. Unlike me, she never had a permanent sense of place. She spent precious little time in the house on the flats and held no affection for it. But that was only part of the problem.

"Mama has had problems ever since I was in grade school. She's spent some time in Orofino."

I was caught unprepared for this revelation. Orofino was and still is the site of State Hospital North, the only publicly funded psychiatric unit in northern Idaho.

"It's my worst fear," Diane repeated, "being like Mama, and being alone."

"Don't worry. Don't you worry," I said. "I won't let that happen to you. I just won't."

I look back on that time now with a humbling sense of futility. How can anyone protect someone else from such fears? How can anyone prevent what may be inevitable?

Alice, after struggling for years to maintain her independence, now lives behind locked doors in the behavioral care unit of a rest home. After visiting my mother-in-law, I now understand the frustration of building a dream without enough Lincoln Logs.

If Diane could only have a house—a real home on land she loved—it would be something her mother hadn't been able to achieve. It would be a place to grow old, a buffer against those overwhelming fears, a familiar environment where, if need be, she could face her own vulnerability.

— • —

Frieda Biggs, a fifty-six-year-old divorcée, helped me better understand Diane's dilemma one day when I arrived with pen in hand, looking for material for my column. She offered a tour of her house as well as her heart.

"We all want to have a sense of place and home," said Frieda, "and you know, when somebody has lived in their home for twenty-five, thirty, maybe forty years, there's a real sense of security. It's traumatic for them to leave."

Frieda reminded me of the people who now tend to the needs of Diane's mother. And in a way, she seemed to know what I was only beginning to grasp about my wife.

"Whether you call it love or affection or whatever, you can't do this kind of work unless you pull people into your heart. I don't know how else to say it."

Frieda lived in Clarkston, Washington, in a house she purchased with her cousin to convert into a licensed family-care home.

"I'm just a caretaker," she said, shrugging off the importance of her work. "Sure, this is what I do for a living. But all my people, I've had them with me for years." Having worked in hospitals, convalescent centers, and rest homes for more than three decades, she said her experiences made her come to grips with a sobering fact of life.

"Unfortunately, we come into the world as babies and sometimes we go out as babies. And we all need loving care, whether it's early in life or late in life."

Patiently putting a client's wispy gray hair up in curlers, she said, "Oh Sophie, you're going to look even more beautiful." Sophie, a frail and elderly woman, lifted her head ever so slowly to reveal an appreciative smile, then bowed and closed her eyes in thought. Two people lived in Frieda's home when I visited her—Sophie and her roommate, Margaret, who was watching television in the living room.

"We put in a big wide window so we have plenty of light," Frieda pointed out as we began touring the house. "And we have a swing outside . . . and of course, here's our bathroom, and the living room, and we have like five doors to go out, which makes it really nice. You know how you've been in homes where you think, 'Oh, I'd better not sit there'? Well, mine is not like that. My home is to be lived in."

At Frieda's feet, three little dogs named Shadow, Muffin, and Billy scampered back and forth in play. "They all needed a home too, and we took them in. They're all strays."

I thought about Flag, one of my old field-trial springer spaniels. We belonged to a program through Washington State University called the People-Pet Partnership. The idea was that dogs, through their unconditional affection for humans, provided a much-needed stimulus for people battling sickness or aging. Flag's and my visits to the rest homes helped me appreciate what a home really is.

Flag loved the weekly routine, I told Frieda. He'd wag his tail the fastest when we went into Art Twist's room. Art suffered—and I really mean suffered—from arthritis. His affliction forced him to be bedridden. His place in the world had become his room.

Art always smiled when Flag and I showed up.

"Hey Flaggy, how ya doin'?" he said. Then Art would motion for me to close the door enough so the nurse couldn't see him invite Flag onto the bed. "Come here, boy."

This was one command Flag never disobeyed. He'd leap right over the bed rail and land almost square on Art's chest with a barrage of licks. Art would raise his crippled hands up to hug the wiggling dog and laugh until I cried. Every time I cried. Not big tears that dribbled down my face, but little ones I'd wipe away in time to lift Flag off the bed before the nurse caught us.

I could almost see myself in the reflection of Art's twinkling eyes, lying there someday—maybe the way Diane saw herself in her mother's eyes.

Then one week, Flag and I went to Art Twist's home to find his place in the world empty.

"He died a few days ago," the nurse said. I could tell she knew about me and my dog and all the fun we'd had with Art.

I never went back to the rest home again. It was too much for me. Flag, like the little dogs I met at Frieda's house, was more than willing to move on to the next room and exchange licks for pats. But I wasn't strong enough. I had given what I could to the lugubrious business of aging. So my appreciation for the home Frieda gave people was sincere.

And then Frieda said something that seemed to strike at the heart of what I wanted to do for Diane. "That's the one thing I hope," Frieda confided, "that someone will take care of me as well as I take care of these people and give me a home."

— • —

About a month after interviewing Frieda, I returned to my childhood home at 1358 Hillcrest Drive, an impromptu deviation from a trip to northern Minnesota. I rented a car at the airport in Minneapolis and drove to Fridley, turned up Woody Lane, then onto Hillcrest Drive, and there it was: the house where I grew up.

I slowly drove past the place. It had been painted light

blue and seemed to have weathered the decades well. The garage door was open, revealing a red car, a motorcycle, and some bikes. Children obviously lived there and I felt good about that. A basketball hoop hung over the garage. I saw myself some thirty-five years ago working on my jump shot in the driveway. I continued on up the hill, which didn't seem nearly as steep as it had in my youth, past the Henkels' house, the Knudsons', the Hansons', the Schillings', back around the loop amid the sunshine and green lawns for a closer look at the old house. This time a woman was sweeping off the front steps. I turned hesitantly into the driveway.

Sue Culbertson welcomed me like a long-lost relative. "Ray has told me all about you and your family," she said. "I'm so glad to meet you." Ray and Betty McAfee still lived next door. I made a note to visit them, but only after I'd taken a peek inside the house.

Sue's thirteen-year-old daughter, Jami, appeared with a basketball under her arm. She'd been playing on the driveway where I learned the game. I should have taken a jump shot but feared I might miss.

The three of us walked through the front door and into the home that housed so many of my memories. Sue and her husband, Terry, had done some remodeling. But for the most part, the house was the same: the little kitchen, the long hallway, my sister's room to the left, then the bathroom, Mom and Dad's room to the right and through this door—the room my brother and I shared, which suddenly looked so *small*.

We toured the basement, the garage, the backyard, the front yard. The trees had grown so big. Jami and I exchanged stories about sledding down the backyard hill with our siblings (she had two sisters and a brother).

I thought about all those old families in the neighborhood. The kids had grown up and, like me, moved elsewhere. A few of the parents, like Ray and Betty and Margaret Knudson, remained. But for all the sameness I found, most everything had changed. In less than an hour, I'd retrieved a big chunk of yesteryear and was overwhelmed by a warm sense of closure, a concession that my old house was now the Culbertsons' home.

When I returned to Idaho, I took an evening walk with the dog out in the field and looked back at our home on the hill. The lights glowed in the windows like they always do. Diane was inside cooking dinner. I thought again about my visit to the house in Fridley, the Culbertsons, and how sometimes it's good to roll back time.

The sound of water spilling out of the pond brought me back to the present. I breathed the fresh mountain air deep into my lungs.

A home is a haven for our souls, where we reside emotionally even when we can't be there physically. All homes, even if you live in seven or more as a child, are shelters amid the press of life's obligations—a place of retreat, warmth, familiarity, and sometimes return.

I'm fortunate finally to get my arms around all that.

CHAPTER THREE

Love, Life's Nectar

What I remember most about our wedding night is that Diane fell asleep.

"Hey," I whispered in her ear, "I love you."

She didn't answer. Exhausted by the day's activities, she lay in bed next to me, her hair flowing down across the pillow, brushing against my face. I breathed deeply, feeding my soul with the fragrance of this young woman who'd so tragically and magically come into my life.

"Do you want to get frisky?"

"Mmmm," she murmured.

For the better part of three years, I wondered if I could ever love again as deeply as I had before. The only thing worse than divorce is an empty marriage, and I'd ended up with both. The former is like open heart surgery—drastic, necessary, and hopefully healing. But the latter is torture—a slow, unrelenting dance with emotional death.

Diane had rescued me from all that. Deep down, she still mourned her first husband's death. But she'd somehow reconciled the loss and opened her arms to me. The least I could do was let her sleep.

The night air drifted across us and I pulled the muslin sheet from our waists up and around her bare shoulders. Diane woke momentarily, turned on her right side, and snuggled backward, rump first, into my body.

"I love you," she whispered sleepily.

"Me too."

I put my left arm around her waist, my fingers against her flat stomach. Then I moved my hand upward beneath the loose top she wore.

"When morning comes, okay?" I said, pulling her even closer.

"Mmmmm," she murmured again.

I was thirty years old. Diane was twenty-five. And we could think of nothing sweeter than growing old together.

— • —

Their love for each other was visible just in the way they hugged. Even the wind chime, decorated with an appropriate red heart, celebrated their embrace as I snapped photos.

They'd married six years earlier and claimed to have "been honeymooning ever since." Posing for a picture was no problem. Just act natural. Hold hands. Smile.

A *love story*, I whispered as the wind chime continued to make music and I tripped the shutter.

Everett Walker, the groom, was seventy-five. His bride, Vivian, was ninety. And their affection for each other was as fresh as they were elderly.

"We're kind of from the old school," said Everett when, notebook in hand, I asked about marriage, aging, and happiness.

"We're perfectly contented and happy. We don't have any differences at all," said Vivian.

And then they hugged again as my camera captured

frame after frame. Almost two decades later, I can still see them standing on the porch in front of their little white house surrounded by shade trees and a well-kept yard. Everett, bald and stooped, wore a plaid shirt with a pocket protector full of pens. Vivian, her hair mussed and white, was brightly attired in a flowered sundress.

Everett readjusted Vivian in his arms and recalled that it was 1971 when each, unknown to the other at the time, began to experience loneliness. "We both lost our mates," said Everett, confiding that the death of his first wife left him devastated. "Every day, life got emptier."

Vivian was more resilient, making the best of being alone. "I got along fine up until I met him," she said, nudging her shoulder toward Everett. "And then I got along finer."

Their meeting was in the cards all along. They found each other one day while sitting at the same pinochle table at the Orofino Senior Citizen Center. The daily games with Vivian sitting nearby, said Everett, perked his interest. Then again, perhaps Vivian stacked the deck.

"One of the neighbors suggested that someone give me and this friend a ride to the center and it fell to his lot," Vivian said, nudging her shoulder toward Everett again. "And that's how it all got started."

They were married in Lewiston and returned to the little white house surrounded by shade trees and the well-kept yard. After twenty-six years on the county highway department, Everett was retired, and he talked about roads as if he'd etched a map in his mind. But mostly, Everett and Vivian talked about their love for each other—and pending vacation plans. Tent-trailer in tow, the two were getting ready to leave for the Grand Canyon, stopping along the way at Pocatello, Idaho, to visit with Vivian's new great-granddaughter.

"If we can't find a campground, we can set up anywhere," said Everett, expounding on the virtues of sleeping in a tent as opposed to motels and such. Vivian nodded agreement. Never-ending honeymoons, they explained, can turn even a KOA campground into a romantic setting.

"As long as we can make it, we'll keep traveling," Everett declared. A spirit of adventure sparked what Everett and Vivian shared. Everything about them seemed if not perfect, as close to it as two people could hope to get.

"Well, if we do have a difference, we can communicate," Everett said. "That's the key."

Then the Walkers stopped holding hands long enough to shake mine, say good-bye, and wave. As I drove off, the wind chime, decorated with the appropriate red heart, made more music in the breeze.

Everett and Vivian seemed to have been made, and then reserved, for each other. They'd loved before and learned late in life that they could love again. They'd experienced so much of life, including the deaths of their previous spouses, that they understood that their newfound companionship would be the compass for the days that remained. They obviously loved each other. But more important, they were *in love*, perhaps beyond "death do us part."

Vivian died on March 22, 1989, of causes related to age. Everett, torn by his bride's passing and ravaged by the cancer he'd fought for years, joined Vivian twenty-two days later.

— • —

Two months after getting married, Diane and I finally went on our honeymoon. Like Everett and Vivian, we were going camping. In early September we left Heidi in the tender care of Grandma Clara and Grandpa Ferd.

"Bye-bye, Kewpie doll," Diane said anxiously, having never been away from Heidi for more than a few hours. And then we were gone, driving in my Datsun 510 with our Kelty backpacks toward the Selway Bitterroot Wilderness Area, up Fog Mountain Road to the trailhead for Cove Lakes and beyond. Just three years earlier, this same backcountry had been a world of transition for me. This is where I had hiked alone to let my heart heal. This is where I cried like the weak man I didn't want to be. This is where a healthy dose of anger eventually built—the kind of ill will a spurned lover needs to sever the ties ultimately, file the legal documents, and make the divorce final.

Diane knew all that. She knew I'd shed some of my past amid the beauty of Idaho's wilderness. But none of it mattered. We were building a new future, together.

"Are you sure we don't need a tent?" Diane asked.

"Naa. We'll sleep under the stars. If it rains, I've got this big poncho. We can bivouac under it."

I could think of nothing more enticing than to share close quarters with Diane. I watched as she trekked in shorts down the trail ahead of me, her long bare legs moving with the rhythm of the terrain and the desire to get to a place where we could be alone.

"Come on. It's so beautiful." Diane seemed determined to lead us to new heights—just like that day months before when she beckoned me up what would become the driveway to our new home.

She broke over the ridge first and I huffed to her side. Off in the distant east, the Selway country stretched far beyond the reach of our eyes—nothing but wilderness for miles. We dumped our packs at our feet and hugged. The afternoon sun shone down and a breeze wrapped us in cooling mountain air. Our hearts were pumping from the exertion and our spirits soared with the excitement only people who climb to mountain peaks can understand.

"And down there," I said, pointing to two sparkling lakes at the base of the ridge we'd climbed, "is our home away from home."

Cove Lakes, despite their remote, high mountain location, rest along one of the more heavily traveled portals into the Selway. The site is a popular destination for day hikers during the summer and offers a splendid prologue or epilogue for those entering or leaving the depths of the wilderness. In September, it's also a dicey place from the standpoint of weather. And by the time Diane and I had hiked down a steep rocky trail into the Cove Lakes basin to set up our honeymoon camp, the day's happy face had turned to a scowl.

I pitched the poncho as rain sprinkled around us. Within half an hour, we were crammed under this sorry excuse for a tent, finishing our freeze-dried supper while trying to make room for our sleeping bags, our equipment, and ourselves.

"I think we're going to get wet."

"You think so?" Diane wisecracked while having the decency to not mention the tent back home.

In fact, for the better part of the next two days we got wet. Fog and rain rolled over us from the ridge above. We ventured outside only for calls of nature and to look up into the kettle gray sky in hope of seeing a break. We read books, sometimes out loud to each other, and we cooked and snacked and shivered and otherwise taxed our young marriage with what was slowly becoming the honeymoon from hell.

Late on the second night, after almost thirty-six hours

under the poncho, with water seeping all around and in some places puddling under us, the rain stopped.

In celebration of this long-awaited cessation, we made love amid the puddles and the clutter that accumulates when two people live under a poncho for two days. Afterward, I lay again on my back with Diane's head nestled upon my shoulder, thinking about how nice it would be to wake up to sunshine and a gloriously warm morning.

About that time, I felt the poncho begin to settle softly down on my face. I pushed up with my hand. The waterproof material felt cold and heavy. I reached out from under the poncho and brought my arm back in with a handful of crystal white flakes.

Snow fell the rest of that night, and by morning's first light, the high country in the Selway Bitterroot Wilderness Area was covered with nearly a foot.

"We've got to get out of here," I said. "We'll dry out as we walk."

"I don't think I *can* walk," replied Diane, rubbing the sore spots on her hips. "That cold ground is awful."

But we did walk up out of the Cove Lakes basin as the temperature rose and the snow melted around us. We picked thumb-sized huckleberries en route to the car and drove home knowing we'd never forget the experience. Later that night, after singing "The Bear Went Over the Mountain" to Heidi, I climbed into bed with Diane. The sheets and blankets were so dry, soft, and warm and we had so much room to spare. You tend to appreciate things like that when you survive a honeymoon under a poncho.

— • —

Some twenty-two years later, Diane and I both look back on our getaway to Cove Lakes and reflect how adversity brought us closer together. That's frequently the case. In my travels for the column I'm often reminded of how many relationships flower amid tragedy and forced separation.

Travis and Betty June Wadley, for example, like so many couples during World War II, found themselves rent asunder by vast oceans and day after day of uncertainty. They longed for each other's touch, but were forced to endure agonizing years apart. Yet, as daunting as it was to experience the horrors of war, the Wadleys agreed that those times were terribly romantic.

"Oh, yes. I think they were," said Betty June. The enforced separation, she suggested, only added to the intensity of feeling.

The Wadleys' romance was more than fifty years old when the two opened a scrapbook and shared their story with me. The heartfelt letters and telegrams pasted on tattered pages lay open the depth of their commitment.

"How is the loveliest little girl in the world?" Travis wrote Betty June from the European front. "Darling, I'd give a million dollars just to see those beautiful big eyes."

The Wadleys had been married just two years when Japan bombed Pearl Harbor. "It was on a Sunday and we heard it on the radio when we were going to his mother's," Betty June recalled. Travis was drafted into the army, became a platoon sergeant in the 385th Engineer General Service Regiment, and was sent to Europe. Betty June moved to Spokane and worked at what is now Fairchild Air Force Base for the war's duration.

The scrapbook, in addition to the love letters and telegrams, also contained newspaper clippings and photographs—all of them prompting memories that the Wadleys yielded openly.

Wire fifty dollars immediately, read the first telegram Travis sent to Betty June on June 18, 1943.

On leave. Having swell time. Wish you were here. Always thinking of and loving you, an August 19, 1943, telegram read.

Sometimes, Travis confided, his love for Betty June was too intense for a telegram that so many others could read. So he wrote letters. "I really poured it on," he said, laughing, while running his fingers over the scrapbook pages.

The timing of my visit with the Wadleys seemed especially appropriate since a cease-fire had just been announced in the Persian Gulf War. Homecomings, the Wadleys said, were one of the few good things about war.

Before Travis came home to Betty June, he participated in the bloody landing at Omaha Beach. As a combat engineer, he was right behind the fighting troops. "When we landed," he wrote, "there were dead soldiers laying all over in the water." The horror and devastation were beyond description, and Travis could do nothing but die or move ahead into the teeth of the German defenses. Months of battle ended when a piece of hot shrapnel ripped through Travis's helmet into the back of his head.

Regret to inform you that your husband Staff Sergeant Travis Wadley was wounded in action eleven Dec. in Belgium, the army wrote in a January 8, 1945, telegram. *You will be advised as reports of condition are received.* The news, said Betty June, left her limp with anguish. She didn't know the extent of her husband's injuries. But she took comfort in knowing he was still alive. Travis was awarded the Purple Heart, recovered in a European hospital, and was shipped home in November.

Several days later, Betty June was waiting for him at the train station in Boise, Idaho, watching as soldier after soldier got off and fell into the arms of loved ones. With each tearful reunion, she grew more anxious.

"I couldn't find my gear," Travis said, explaining why he

was last off the train. And when he did finally step down into sight he was at the far end of the cars.

"So I did a little running," Betty June said, blushing. And yes, there was that predictable leap into each other's arms and a kiss that seemed never to end. Jested Travis, "I swear, our first daughter was born nine months and fifteen minutes after I got home."

— • —

I've always fancied carving our initials in a tree: *D. J. + D. J.* Diane and I talked about it many times, but never got around to it. One winter, however, I came close.

A snowstorm swept through the region and left a fresh six inches or more on a landscape that was already covered with winter's white blanket. I donned snowshoes and tramped into our woods, then high-stepped over the fence into the neighbor's open field. Like sand in the desert, the snow had drifted across the field and deposited on the leeward side of a hill facing our home. Inspired by the clean expanse, I stomped through the snowbank, down and around again until I'd spelled I-L-O-V-E-Y-O-U. By the time I finished an hour later, perspiration had frozen to my mustache and beard. But I never felt warmer.

Job complete, I went back over the hill, across the field, straddled the fence, and hustled back through the woods toward home. Before going in the back door, I swept my feet clean, then walked inside, hung my coat up, and rushed to the dining room window to observe my work.

Diane had already seen it. She was standing at the window with a steaming cup of tea in her hands and a charmed grin on her face.

"Me too," she said, putting down the cup and opening her arms. I moved briskly to her and looked over her shoulder to the field beyond. Just enough sunlight had broken through the clouds to cast shadows across the snow and put the words in boldface.

"I love you," I said, both reading what I'd written and voicing what I felt.

— • —

Randy Knight, like me, was a hopeless romantic. Unlike me, he also had a proclivity for the stage. When he was a young boy growing up in the Lewiston-Clarkston Valley, he would sometimes hold a short section of hose near his mouth, put the other end to his ear, and sing "Love Me Tender."

"I'd practice hours and hours trying to get the inflections down," the forty-seven-year-old Randy told me when I arrived for another column interview one day. He also sang Beatles and Rolling Stones songs and otherwise occupied his days with music of the fifties and sixties.

"I've always been in love with rock 'n' roll," Randy admitted, emphasizing the words "in love."

At the time we talked, he'd recently fallen deeply in love with Julie Perrigo, a thirty-seven-year-old divorced mother of three who tended bar at the Der Litten Haus tavern in Clarkston, Washington. The bar, in fact, is where Randy and Julie met, she serving drinks and he performing onstage.

"He doesn't only impersonate Elvis," said Julie, who joined the conversation in Randy's apartment. "He also does a real good Jack Nicholson."

"Well, thank you, honey, thank you very much," Randy said, acknowledging his fiancée's compliment in his best Elvis voice.

Julie was the furthest thing from a "groupie." The way

she looked at Randy betrayed her feelings: She loved him both for who he was and for what he wanted to be.

I wondered if Elvis/Jack/Randy had ever thought about getting a day job.

"Oh, yes," said Randy. A high school dropout, he had worked at a number of different professions. Having also struggled with a number of ailments, Randy described himself as a semi-retired entertainer who'd come to grips with not having made it to the big time. And Julie didn't mind at all—she loved his quirky multiple personalities.

"Well, when you've got Elvis, or maybe even Kirk Douglas in your life, it's pretty interesting." Loving Randy, Julie said, meant loving his music, and both had swept her away.

On cue, Randy reintroduced the performing side of his personality. "Sometimes I'm Kirk Douglas, looking in the refrigerator. . . . I just want to be free. Or I impersonate Jimmy Carter doing Stevie Wonder. Well, I don't do any songs, but I do eat peanuts."

Having performed in a number of groups over the years, Randy said he preferred to be a "one-man band." He played guitar and for his show had prerecorded percussion and keyboard accompaniment. His repertoire included about twenty-five Elvis songs.

"And 'Pretty Woman' by Roy Orbison," he said, looking at Julie.

At the time, Randy was getting ready to do some crooning at a woman's fiftieth-birthday bash. "Those little old ladies love it," Julie put in.

"It's better to be good and appreciated than to be rich and not so appreciated," Randy reasoned. "Look how unhappy Elvis was when he died."

Eight months after we talked, Randy woke one morning and complained to Julie about indigestion. He'd been having problems for some time and was taking antacid pills that provided only marginal relief. Pushing himself through the discomfort, he donned his Elvis clothes that night and performed at a local tavern, returning home about 2:30 A.M.

Julie woke some three hours later to find Randy lying dead in the kitchen, the victim of a massive heart attack.

"He had a bad heart," she said. "I think he knew it."

The irony, of course, was that Randy had a good heart. Julie knew it better than anyone. The two had planned to be married the following spring. "The week before he died it was my birthday and we had such a good time. I was pretty devastated. I really miss him a lot."

I talked with Julie again, some two years after Randy's death. She was still hurting and concluded that nothing hurts like the sudden death of a lover. I understood something of what she was feeling. Diane had lost Stan just as suddenly, and I'd watched her deal with that pain.

"I've learned a lot," Julie said. "I've learned that when you love someone, you can't take that for granted, because you don't know what will happen. I just know that he loved me too."

And as for the future!

"I think when I come out of my shell, I'll find someone . . . or maybe they'll find me." She said there was something trite but profoundly true in the line "Better to have loved and lost than never to have loved at all." Knowing that, Julie said, made it worth trying to love again.

— • —

Of course, for every maxim there's an exception. I met at least one woman who loved, lost, and couldn't have cared less about loving again.

Florie Mullikin, who answered her telephone just before

Valentine's Day, figured Cupid could take his bow and arrow and shoot himself in the foot.

"I hate the holiday because I hate making out all those stupid cards," said Florie.

Might it be worth taking on the chore if there were a prospect in sight?

"At this point in life, I just don't have anybody," she declared. Not that she didn't see value in loving relationships. "I know some people who are just meant for each other and they've had perfect marriages for twenty or twenty-five years," she said. "But I feel sorry for gals and guys who feel they have to have a soul mate."

Florie worked at the Strike and Spare Bar and Grill in downtown Lewiston, Idaho. She was a cook. "The only passion in my life has been cooking," she said. "I love to cook. Sometimes, that's all I think about.

"Don't get me wrong," Florie assured. "I like guys . . . for a three-day weekend and then I'm tired of them."

A twice-divorced mother of five, Florie said her marriages were good while they lasted and she's never faulted the two men she used to call husbands. "They're really good guys. But I'm just not cut out to be married. You can ask almost anyone who knows me. I'm the most anti-marriage person there is. When I hear somebody is getting married, I say, 'Oh, can I talk you out of it?' "

While soured on matrimony, Florie admitted that her heart did occasionally go aflutter. She read romance novels and considered the best-selling *The Bridges of Madison County* the ultimate tale of love. "I don't cry, but that book made me cry. I guess I like reading about love. It looks good on paper."

What she really loved, even more than popular fiction, was freedom. "I'm the last of the hippies. I'm just too independent, I guess. I'm probably what you'd call a female chauvinist. I get along well alone. I can eat crackers in bed and read all night if I want. I don't have to listen to country western music. I can listen to rock all I want. I still like ZZ Top the best."

Exercising such independence meant bucking criticism from the rest of society. Despite a divorce rate that continues to soar, the world was still a "coupled" place, she said. "But you don't have to do what society tells you. If you're comfortable and secure with yourself, you don't need another person." Then again, she conceded, there was still a chance "Mr. Right" might someday address a big red Valentine to her.

As it turned out, Florie received no Valentines. *"Nada!"* she said. "And you told me everyone, after reading my story, would send me flowers."

Just as well, she said. "I just can't imagine getting married anyway. I love doing what I want."

Independence is seductive. Yet one wonders how compatible it is with love. The majority of us depend on one another for emotional well-being and reckon the reward of a feeling of wholeness with the sacrifice of a little bit of autonomy.

— • —

When Diane and I stood before the minister on our wedding day, we took vows that included the words "in sickness and in health." I took the phrase seriously, but admit I didn't fully appreciate its importance.

Rick and Roberta Kruger, on the other hand, started their marriage by testing that part of their commitment— Roberta from the confines of a wheelchair.

The Krugers, of Troy, Idaho, had been teenage sweethearts when, on Christmas Eve in 1984, Roberta experienced the first symptom. A grayish object seemed to be floating in her peripheral vision. She read some medical books and became terrified.

"I thought, oh no, glaucoma. And I panicked."

She and Rick had been dating since high school. "I've still got my promise ring," Roberta told me when I interviewed her.

Rick graduated a year before Roberta. They were in love and were determined to make sure Roberta's "pesky ailments," which by then had developed beyond the vision problem, didn't ruin their plans. It was two years later when Roberta, still plagued with physical problems, made another doctor's appointment.

"We'd already set our wedding date," said Roberta. Then came the diagnosis.

Multiple sclerosis.

"Rick was in the room with me and we just looked at each other and said, 'What's that?'" recalled Roberta. "Even when the doctor said I had it, it still didn't mean that much to us."

Looking back, the couple thinks the doctor spared them the details in deference to the wedding plans they'd already made in the anticipation of moving overseas.

"Rick joined the army and we went to Germany and we had a heck of a time over there," said Roberta. But now and then, she recalled, there were little things, like a tingling sensation in her fingers. "I didn't think much of it. I even had a job over there."

The Krugers also had their first child, Kevin, in Germany and three years later moved back to Spokane, Washington. Rick was discharged from the service and the young family moved to Sandpoint, Idaho, where Rick, drawing on his experience in the army as a power-generator repairman, built new generators for a private company. Matthew, the

Krugers' second son, was born after they moved to Troy, Idaho, in 1991. Rick was working for Strom Electric, and suddenly, in the summer of 1992, Roberta took a turn for the worse.

"I really got depressed," she said. "I figured, this is it. I'm going to die."

Multiple sclerosis, otherwise known as MS, is a disease that attacks the central nervous system and can cause partial or complete paralysis. Roberta began having difficulty walking. Then she started to fall.

"Rick had to hold me up," she said. "But the thought of using a cane was unacceptable." Eventually she relented to the cane, then a walker. And just four months before I visited the family, a wheelchair became part of Roberta's life.

"I was just falling so much and I have three kids," she explained. The Krugers' third child, Carissa, was just two years old. Being a stay-at-home mom in a wheelchair tested Roberta and her family.

"Every day is a challenge," said Rick. Medicaid helped pay for Roberta's medical bills and some of the in-home assistance she received. Rick hoped to find a home for his family closer to work.

"There are a lot of times I get down," admitted Roberta. But her children helped prop her up both physically and emotionally. Not only did they love her back, but they also needed their mom. And so far she'd been able to keep up with them in the wheelchair.

"It was so gradual," she said of the disease's development. "You more or less grow into it. But it did take me a year to accept it."

Being pregnant with Carissa was perhaps the biggest challenge. Roberta fell several times during the pregnancy but managed to protect her abdomen. "I kept telling her [Carissa], 'I'm going to get you into the world somehow.'"

Carissa was born on January 17, 1995.

Rick said he and his wife held out no false hope. "They haven't found anything for chronic progressive MS," he said. But Roberta was sanguine that more research would be done on methods to help restore the central nervous system. "You don't know what the future holds, so we take one day at a time," she said.

It was more than two years before I got around to checking in with the Krugers again. Roberta said her illness was about the same but that, even if it got worse, she wouldn't notice.

Rick certainly noticed.

"It tears at you. She used to go huntin' and fishin' with me, really share in it. And now she can't walk."

Roberta's limitations were something neither she nor Rick had fully envisioned when they were courting, of course. "We were in love," Roberta said. "So the thought of breaking up, when the doctor said I had MS, was just ridiculous. We were teenagers and figured, well, who thinks they're going to be bound to a wheelchair?"

Also entering into the equation were the three children they'd brought into the world.

"That's our responsibility, to raise them. And it's hard on the kids," said Rick. "It's put a big load on them, because they're her legs when I'm not home."

I was interested in probing Rick's thoughts. Had he *ever* experienced moments of doubt about his future with Roberta?

After a couple moments of silence, Rick answered as best he could. "When I said 'I do,' I meant it. I've often been asked that question—heard something like 'Most guys would have left.' I suppose if I hadn't had a really good upbringing, I wouldn't have accepted the responsibility. But you got to just suck it up and move on. That's what Roberta does."

Then Rick hesitated. "Gosh," he said, "you're making me think more than I have in a long time."

He reflected a few seconds more.

"It takes a bigger man to stand there and fight for what you believe in and love than it does to just walk away," he said finally. "If you've got something you love, why throw it away?"

— • —

Sometimes, when Diane and I are at odds, I'm awed by how strong our love must be. The truth is, we occasionally have a difficult time getting along. Neither of us has ever capitulated to the other's dominant personality. And even though we share so many of the same ideas and values, we look at the world in different ways. I'm pretty much a big-picture person who sees a black-and-white landscape of simple daily decisions, few of which are worthy of second thought. Diane, on the other hand, is a detail person who sees her environment as a kaleidoscope of Technicolor options, all of which warrant her focused attention.

I don't know why two people like us fall in love. Maybe opposites do attract. But I'm too impatient to probe such an idea and Diane would consider our love too important to explain away with a shallow aphorism. Neither of us wants to fool anybody into thinking we're the ideal couple. At times, we can drive each other nuts.

There does, however, remain a nectar in our life—a sweet feeling not just of loving each other, but of being in love. I know it when she finally hugs me after a fight. I know it even more when we share the many things we love together—like our daughters and our home.

The key, of course, is to stay truly in love. It's quite possible to continue loving someone, even though you're not "in love," to remain together out of respect for a relationship that has produced mostly good times. But that taste is bland. The never-ending challenge, therefore, is to forbid the bad times from tainting the sweet taste we cherish so much.

That's why I was so gratified to meet Tom and Mary Kiiskila, who hadn't just stayed in love but had made sure to drink every last drop of the nectar they could.

Not to mention a little moonshine now and then.

The first thing Tom said when I called was, "Ya, come talk with us. I'll heat up the sauna."

I drove into the older, eastern end of Orofino, Idaho, and was pleased to discover that Mary also used to do a lot of driving for a living. During bootlegging days, she piloted her '27 Dodge over the back roads to Spokane. There, she'd load up with moonshine and smuggle the hooch back to the White Hotel in Orofino.

"There were stills in the woods all over the place," said Mary, who was an energetic eighty-six years old. "But we could buy better moonshine in Spokane, so that's why we went there."

Tom, Mary's husband of forty-five years, took a sauna every week. He showed me the cedar-lined bathhouse first thing after introductions.

"We can fire 'er up," he offered.

I declined. Then I told Tom that my mother's uncle Everett had a sauna and my dad, Roy, would sit in the thing until the sweat was running down around his ankles and he looked like he was melting away. Then Dad, who weighed more than 250 pounds, would exit the sauna, lumber down to the dock, and gracefully dive headfirst into the lake. I'd watch the waters part and marvel at his big white body sliding beneath the surface of the coffee-brown water away from the dock, farther and farther, until he surfaced on his back and spouted water out of his mouth like a big whale.

"Ya, ya." Tom, who was even bigger than my dad, grinned. "So, you say your dad, he was part Finn?"

Disappointed as he was when he realized Dad Johnson was all Swede, no Finn, Tom kind of reminded me of my dad. He liked a good joke and tended to fill in the gaps when his wife left the good parts out of a story.

"Mary, she was bootlegging in Spokane," he said as we walked back into the kitchen, "and they said, 'Why don't you go to Orofino?'" Tom was fourteen years younger than Mary and apparently figured any story worth telling had to have a good beginning followed by a better ending.

"Ya, so she started up there," he said, looking at Mary as if his words were a cue for her to pick up the plot.

Mary lifted an eyebrow like she'd had enough of Tom's befuddled attempt to get the chronology right and then asserted, "Whiskey wasn't legal then . . . because you got the license for the place when I lost it."

"Well, I used to go to Clarkston to get the whiskey," Tom said, scratching his bald head.

"We're getting old"—Mary sighed—"so we don't remember everything."

"That was before slot machines became legal," piped in Tom, having sifted a few more facts and dates into order. "Ya, we had slot machines too."

"We should have wrote a book," said Mary.

Tom and Mary Kiiskila were, if not the stuff of oral history projects, candidates for standup comedy. Their version of yesteryear was punctuated with lighthearted banter and muddled memories. They still owned the White Hotel. It was a two-story rooming house for bachelors that was indeed painted white and stood tall in the timber town's former red-light district.

"The cat house used to be right over there," Tom said with a wink while pointing out the window.

In addition to their recollections and the weekly sauna, I quickly found out that Tom and Mary were also willing to share their moonshine.

"Alcohol. Just plain alcohol," said Mary, pulling a bottle from the shelf and offering a swig.

I flashed back to my college days when we used to pass around wine bottles during all-night cram sessions.

"Ya, ya!" Tom coached.

I pulled the cork and threw back a snort.

"Hey, hey, hey," Mary snickered as the crystal-clear liquid singed its way toward my innards. "You can say you tasted real moonshine. That's why we have it."

My eyes watered. My ears burned. My voice struggled to return as I inquired about mixers.

"Nope. Just straight," declared Tom. "That way it sticks with ya."

Drinking a few beers on the job is sometimes necessary in my kind of work. But pouring straight alcohol into my system might interfere with the interview process. So I corked the jug, carefully shuttled it back into Mary's waiting arms, and watched her stow it on the kitchen counter within arm's reach. Then, as if the liquor had loosened *their* tongues instead of mine, Finn Mary and Tom launched into autobiographies.

Mary talked of her life on the Great Plains, of grasshoppers that chased her family from the farming country of mid-America to Spokane (where she began bootlegging), of two husbands who died, and of coming to Orofino in 1929 and buying the White Hotel with another woman whose husband later shot her in a murder-suicide.

Tom, who was born in Virginia, Minnesota, came to the Clearwater country of Idaho in 1936 as a logger. He became part of Mary's life in the wake of her second husband's death.

"We buried him in Lewiston," Mary recalled. After the funeral, she wasn't feeling up to driving her Dodge back to Orofino. So she turned to Tom, who, along with many other loggers, had attended the burial.

"I said, 'Get in here and drive this car,' and he's been driving ever since," Mary said. "I told him when he got me I was a sticker and he'd never get rid of me."

"I couldn't see what she seen in me. All I had was a sack full of dirty socks," Tom said.

But the two weathered the Great Depression together, even those times when Idaho, despite the repeal of prohibition nationwide, continued to ban the sale of hard liquor.

"Senseless law, anyways," scoffed Mary. Everybody, she and Tom claimed, served behind closed doors. All of which reminded Tom of a good story. There was a time during those state prohibition years, he said, when Clearwater County got a new sheriff and prosecutor. The two decided to dry up the wet spots in Orofino, including the White Hotel.

Tom, clad in a plaid shirt and suspenders, needed to settle deeper into his chair to tell this particular story. He put his elbows on the table and leaned into the heart of the yarn with his eyes dancing. I realized I wasn't the first to hear the account and probably wouldn't be the last.

"This new sheriff and prosecutor, they were both deacons in the church," he began. The two officials were quite high and mighty, according to Tom, and it was only a matter of time before the authorities caught him with ten cases of illegal whiskey.

"They come and raided us," Tom said. The sheriff, apparently acting on a tip from some teetotaler or a talkative drunk, confiscated the cases of booze and carried them out to his squad car. Then he returned and asked if there was more hooch on the premises. That's when Tom decided it was time to put one over on the law and in the process realized the advantage of being bilingual.

He began speaking Finnish to a hotel patron sitting nearby. "I told him 'When we go back in the cooler, you fellers clean that whiskey out of the police car.'" Well, Tom rummaged around in the cooler and stalled the sheriff and prosecutor long enough for the evidence in the back of the squad car to disappear mysteriously.

"So I pleaded not guilty," laughed Tom. "It pays to talk two languages."

Always on cue, Mary grabbed the jug and this time all three of us took a snort.

I coughed and muttered something about the moonshine "sticking."

The Kiiskilas, like all people, had their share of problems. But instead of dwelling on them, they made light of themselves and their circumstances. Clearly the old "someone who makes me laugh" standard made their marriage "stick," and I think if more couples were as quick to find humor in everything as Tom and Mary, the divorce rate would drop by half. Although, come to think of it, the bootlegging rate might double.

Tom died two years later. We never did do the sauna. Shortly after Tom's passing, Mary moved to Coeur d'Alene, Idaho, to live for some seven years with her daughter-in-law. She was ninety-five when I talked with her again.

"I'm still kickin' around," she said, her voice struggling to restore the levity I'd heard before.

Mary died two years after that. I can still hear her and Tom laughing in their kitchen. I smile every time I think about that day. I also can't help comparing their relationship to Diane's and mine.

It took about two weeks for me to fall fully in love. But it's taken me nearly two decades to understand that a relationship fails when lovers lose sight of what made them fall for each other in the first place: the humor, the fun, the joy in just being together. Too many people believe in constantly leaping off romantic cliffs for the sake of drama when what they really need for romance to stay alive is a series of small, soft landings. We must find little ways to keep falling in love, lest we fall out of it.

So yes, it is time again to go rub Diane's feet and whisper those words in her ear. Or maybe I'll just mow the lawn without waiting for her to ask.

CHAPTER FOUR

Kids, Moms, and Dads

Carl Melina waited to catch Levi.

Diane was ready to deliver.

I tried to be brave and remember my coaching lessons from Lamaze class.

"One more push," moaned Diane.

"Okay, one more," said Carl, patiently sitting at the foot of the bed with his arms folded across his chest. We called him Carl instead of Doctor because he was as much a friend as he was our family physician.

"Just one more," Diane wheezed as her body went into yet another isometric contortion.

I was propped behind her on the hospital bed, trying to support Diane's back while looking down over her shoulder at the stomach that had grown to pumpkin size in nine months. We knew it was going to be a boy. We weren't really hoping for a son as much as we just knew it. We'd even started calling him Levi. The name was old-fashioned and, to my way of thinking, had a ring of athleticism about it. Levi "White Shoes" Johnson, destined to play wide receiver in the National Football League.

"Aaaaaah!" my wife suddenly roared. The sound seemed to come from some cavernous maternal recess that women can tap only when giving birth and men can remotely understand only if they've taken their Lamaze lessons to heart.

"Levi's coming," I shouted as Carl scrambled and Diane lay her head back on my shoulder to deal with the final throes of delivery. I looked down and couldn't believe my eyes. The pumpkin was sliding out of my wife's body on the day before Halloween in 1980. Trick-or-treat cigars were in the offing for all my buddies, even the women, in the newsroom.

Diane lifted her head to monitor Carl's work. "One, two, three," he counted as he unwrapped the umbilical cord from around the baby's neck. I saw a little scrunched-up face, and then little arms and hands as Diane coasted toward the delivery of our son.

"It's a girl!"

"It's a girl. It's Greta," Diane said, confirming the doctor's diagnosis.

I paused, took a look for myself, and just that fast fell in love with the daughter I knew we were going to have all along.

"Greta," I said. "You surprised us. How are you?"

But Greta didn't answer. She didn't cry. She made no sounds. She rolled her eyes once and then didn't move. Carl quickly cut the umbilical cord and she lay limp across his hands. Our doctor seemed to be juggling our daughter into the world, moving her back and forth between his hands in search of life. He turned quickly toward an oxygen machine across the room. Diane and I were momentarily frozen in time, sweat still clinging to her body, fright beginning to contort my face.

And then we heard the cry, comfortingly loud and demanding.

"What time is it?" asked Diane.

"A little after midnight."

"Good," she said, welcoming the product of our love into her arms. It was October thirtieth. Greta had been born on her Grandpa John's birthday.

"Grandpa will be happy," I told our baby as she suckled Diane's breast.

That night in the Gritman Memorial Hospital birthing room, my weary wife and I took turns holding our new daughter. Diane nursed Greta and tried to sleep. I marveled at our baby's beauty and had never felt more awake. Heidi was waiting at Grandma Clara's house to meet her new sister. We called with the news and couldn't wait to get the girls together.

Twelve hours later, when we got to Grandma's, Diane sat down and opened the warm blanket for everyone to see the newest member of our family.

Heidi peeked inside, looked up at us, and said, "Where's Levi?"

— • —

While Greta needed coaxing to give her lungs a workout, Matthew Becker seemed to require no urging at all. I heard him crying in the background as his mother answered the phone. Two days after his birth, it seemed Matthew was still trumpeting the wonder of it all, and I was struck with inspiration: What if I interviewed Matthew?

When I met Matthew a couple days later, he was snoozing the afternoon away in his bassinet in front of a big picture window. Outside, the world was awash in golden stubble fields that surrounded the Becker family farmhouse near Colton, Washington. The harvest was over. It was late October, the same time of year when Greta was born, and the aspen trees outside Matthew's big picture window were shedding their yellow cloak.

"What a life," an exhausted Lori whispered while nudging Matthew's bassinet. "The little stinker, he gets to sleep."

I looked admiringly at the newest Becker child and touched his cheek with my little finger. Matthew had already taken his first bath, soiled several diapers, and cried just enough to make sure no one forgot him. Sometimes, as if sensing winter around the corner, Matthew squirmed under his blue blanket and made snuggling sounds like a puppy searching for warmth amid the litter.

"He's such a good baby," cooed Mom, delivering the love-blind assessment all moms can be counted on to give.

When Dad held Matthew, Mike Becker's big farmer hands seemed to cradle all that was important in the world.

"Hi dude," said Mike as Matthew yawned and opened his eyes just long enough to sneak a peek at what the commotion was all about.

"His eyes are blue," said Lori.

"He already smiles," insisted Mike. Art lovers gazing upon the *Mona Lisa* could not have worn expressions more admiring.

For the Beckers, parents of four, it seemed that nurturing children went hand in hand with cultivating crops. Once again I was reminded that few ties are stronger than the one that binds generations on a family farm.

"You hope for the best. That's all you can do," Mike said of his son's future.

Matthew had already visited one set of grandparents in Moscow; his paternal grandparents paid a call shortly after Matthew came home from the hospital; and he met his aunt and six-year-old cousin soon after. But all that visiting was nothing compared to the socializing Matthew and his brother and sisters had been doing. Andy, six, liked to comb Matthew's hair. Christy, four, helped change diapers. Katie, two, was in charge of hugs and kisses.

"We'll probably take him with us when we go up on the butte to check the cattle," Lori said of Matthew's most imminent adventure. Also in his future were donning a costume as the family's youngest Halloween goblin, baptism at Saint Gall's Catholic Church, learning to say "Mama" before saying "Daddy," and finding a niche amid sibling rivalry.

"He's such a good baby," Mom reminded me, careful to make sure her son got good press right from the start.

And then Lori let me hold him. I nestled Matthew's butt in the palm of my right hand and cradled his head in the left. Then I shifted his little body around and held him close to my heart, the way people always do when they take children into their arms. I snuggled him close and he made me think back to that earlier October day when Greta surprised us all.

Moms and dads don't really care whether their kids come into the world as boys or girls. Oh sure, maybe there's some consternation about the purchase of pink or blue blankets and discussion about alternative names like Levi or Greta. But what's really important is that you suddenly have this little person in your arms who's healthy and wiggly and totally dependent on your unconditional love.

— • —

I often wonder if kids realize we're telling the truth when we say it seems like time flies. I blinked and my baby girl was walking with her big sister Heidi. I blinked again and she was competing in college track meets. Like all parents, I sometimes wish I could go back and see that sweet little girl who used to fly kites and listen to me like I knew everything.

"Can I tug it?" asked Greta.

"Just a minute. I need to make sure it stays up. Sometimes kites fall down."

"Oh."

We lay in the green pasture grass, my five-year-old daughter and I, as the breeze brushed over the top of us and I slowly let the string uncoil. The kite climbed higher and higher as Greta's eyes grew wider and wider.

"I hope Mom sees it," she said.

"Oh, I'm sure she can. Look, she's looking out the window right now." Greta boosted herself up to a sitting position and waved. Diane stood in the dining room of our home, craning her neck toward the sky to watch the kite suspended high above the hay field.

"Can I tug it now?" said Greta. "I want to hold it."

"Okay. It's your turn."

Earlier that morning, after Heidi boarded the bus for school, Greta had come stumbling down the steps from her bedroom with her new kite.

"It's windy, Dad."

"Oh, but I have to go to work and write stories."

"You said we could fly it when it got windy."

"But, I'm supposed to . . . ah, okay. But just for a while."

"Be fun," said Greta.

"You're right. It will be fun."

So there we were, feeding the multicolored kite up into the sky, doing nothing productive except enjoying the springtime day and each other.

"When I was a kid," I said, "we flew kites in Minnesota, where the March wind always roared like a lion."

"Mmmm," said Greta. "Talk more 'bout Minnesota."

"Oh, the kids in our neighborhood, we used to fly maybe six kites at once in the field behind Billy Schilling's house. We'd lie in the grass, just like we're doing now, and eat peanut butter and jelly sandwiches and talk about stuff."

"I like peanut butter and jelly, mmmm," said Greta.

"Mmmm, me too."

I let the moment consume my thoughts and being.

"One time," I continued, "Kevin Knudson wanted to write naughty words on his kite. But Billy said no way. His mom would see the kite no matter where we flew it."

"Can we have peanut butter and jelly for lunch?"

"Sure."

A gust of wind whipped through the bare aspen tree branches behind us and tripped my memory further.

"We had giant kite-eating oak trees when I was a kid."

"How do you mean?"

"Well, every now and then," I said, "when you least expected it, the wind would push your kite off to the side and a big oak tree would just reach right out and grab it."

"Uh-uh," Greta said, "trees don't grab."

"Oh yes they did. And when they did, that was it for your kite. When you tried to pull it down, the string would break. And then, when summer came, the leaves grew thick and the kite would disappear, like it had been eaten up. And sure enough, when winter came and the leaves fell, there would be what was left of your kite . . . just a skeleton tangled up in the branches."

Greta giggled because she knew Dad was telling another story. Then we just lay there silently—two kids looking up at the beautiful kite dancing in the sky.

For Greta, it was a moment that would become a memory. For me, it was a chance to let my imagination soar, just

for a few moments, beyond the tethers of work and responsibility.

Fortunately, though, the column brings me in touch
with all ages and sorts, from baby Matthew to great-grand-
mothers to five-year-old Lee Ann Humble-Fotheringham,
who didn't have a kite but possessed an imagination that
had no trouble taking flight. She had a toy box in the living room, a computer in the kitchen, a babbling brook in
her backyard, and a dog named Popeye almost always at
her side.

Lee Ann also had a doll named Norma and said she
couldn't wait to "go on the fast road" in a school bus to
kindergarten. What's more, she could click and drag her
way through cyberspace at a pace that left me scratching
my head.

A pint-sized master of non sequiturs, Lee Ann told me
she'd cut her hair "because it was down in my eyes," and
she also pointed out that she'd given Popeye's tail a trim.

"And guess what?" she whispered conspiratorially. "I
walked barefoot through the stream and found a frog under
a rock.

"And Mommy found a big one, and I found another big
one, 'cept Daddy found the biggest one. I don't know."

Lee Ann was the daughter of Debbie Humble and Jerry
Fotheringham. The family lived in what many people
might describe as a run-down house in need of improve-
ments of the sort Lee Ann's parents couldn't afford. Perhaps fifty or more years old, the house was propped against
the north slope of the Clearwater River canyon at the west
edge of the tiny town of Greer, Idaho. Some eighteen
months earlier, the babbling brook in Lee Ann's backyard
couldn't handle the spring runoff from the mountains and
a huge mudslide almost swept the house, Lee Ann, and her
parents away.

"A log came in," Lee Ann said. "It didn't scare me. It scared Mommy and Daddy. And Popeye, he was sleeping in the bathroom upstairs and the mud didn't come in there."

The house bore the scars of the ordeal and there was so much work ahead, lamented Jerry and Debbie. But both credited their little girl for getting everyone through the experience and looking to the future again.

"She keeps us going in more ways than one," said Jerry. "We'd have given up last year if it wasn't for her. She keeps sparking us along."

Lee Ann seemed as intrigued with me as I was with her. She took my hand and together we began to explore her world of play. The toy box was her first stop.

"This stuff got dirty in the mud," Lee Ann apologized, sorting through the first layer of toys. "This is a new piggy bank Daddy bought me," she said, digging deeper into the treasures. "I lost the pink piggy bank."

Norma, Lee Ann's doll, also happened to be resting in the toy box. Lee Ann snatched up the doll, gave it a kiss, tucked it under her arm, and continued to sort. "This is a little chick, and here's a kitty. Its name is Tee Why."

After getting to the bottom of the toy box and playing with the ingredients for a few minutes, Lee Ann announced that her newest toy was "in the computer. You know, CDs are compact discs." With that, she escorted me to the kitchen table, where a computer sat, looking incongruous with Lee Ann's humble surroundings. With Norma in her left hand and the computer mouse in her right, Lee Ann peered into the monitor and began clicking away.

"Putt-Putt travels through time," she said as the words came on the screen.

On top of her computer savvy she could read too?

Jerry explained that his daughter seemed to know her way around the computer as if she could read every word.

"I like to play with the computer," said Lee Ann. "I like Putt-Putt, 'cause we bought it and I have fun on it. Putt-Putt just rolls around and talks. . . . See?"

Lee Ann clicked on the little car's mouth.

"Mr. Firebird is expecting us," said Putt-Putt. "Click on the road and off we go."

Lee Ann clicked on the road. "Yikes," she squealed, "I almost ran over the cow."

I asked if Norma liked computers too.

"Oh no." Lee Ann giggled. "She's just a dolly."

But Norma and the other dolls in her toy box liked to play in the water, said Lee Ann, suddenly popping the Putt-Putt disc out of the computer, shutting down the equipment, and retreating to the backyard. I grabbed my camera and followed. There, in a Styrofoam cooler anchored in the little stream, floated about eight dolls and a teddy bear.

"I put them in there so I could clean them. They got dirty. They're just floating. Well, I like to sit in there and play with them," said Lee Ann.

When she gets big, said Lee Ann, she planned to "be a, be a . . . I don't know."

Her dad, quite predictably, seemed pleased with everything about Lee Ann, including her indecision about a career. "We just want to give her every chance she can get. We just let her roll. She's pretty independent."

With that, Lee Ann scampered back into the house with Norma.

"Bye-bye."

As I watched her disappear, I thought about Greta, whose main priority used to be peanut butter and jelly, kites, and her dad's tales of Minnesota. I hoped that Jerry and Debbie would appreciate how little time would pass before Lee Ann would have the option of *programming* computers instead of just playing on them.

— • —

Of course, one of my daughters entered my life not through the wonder of birth, but on the heels of tragedy. I must admit, I wrestled with whether Heidi really needed a step-dad in her life, or just the warm image of the father that her family kept alive.

"Do you remember your Daddy Stan?" I asked Heidi on Father's Day when she was five.

"Mom has a picture," she said. "And I can see him in my head."

I'd queried Heidi about Stan before, but on this day we were getting ready to visit the Rock Creek Cemetery and I felt a need for some clarity. She was getting older and I wondered how often she grappled with her dad's death, and how she'd come to view the loss.

Earlier in the morning, Heidi had ventured out to pick a bouquet of wildflowers from the edge of the woods and fields around our house. She put lupine and Indian paint-brush in an empty honey can and Mom filled it with water.

"Don't spill," Diane said to Heidi while looking at me to make sure I got the same message.

Heidi and I drove on, over and around the dusty gravel roads, past fields of hay and green grain drenched in sun-light.

"I see Daddy Stan up there right now, driving a race car," Heidi said, pointing to the sky. "That cloud looks like a race car."

I laughed. So did Heidi.

The cemetery sat atop a knoll about three miles south of Potlatch, Idaho. In the spring it's a peaceful, grassy place shaded by big fir trees and overlooking the Hoodoo Mountains to the east. Gold Hill, where Stan died and where Diane, Heidi, and I met, rests to the north. Moscow Mountain is to the south. Birds seem never to stop singing.

Heidi learned the way to Daddy Stan's grave about the time she started walking. And as I watched her skipping off through the headstones on this day, I was resigned to saying nothing, to letting her handle the scene in her five-year-old way.

"Oh gee, there's a grasshopper," she said, chasing the bug around and around in the grass. Then she transferred her flowers from the honey can to a vase and poured the water.

"Full," she said as the water trickled over the lip of the vase.

Diane designed Stan's headstone. A picture of him riding his horse is etched on the face.

"There's Pepper, right there," Heidi said.

Then she was off picking wild roses from along the fence line around the cemetery. She placed three on the grave, looked at her arrangement, adjusted two of the flowers, balanced on one foot, sighed, and said, "I could eat a thousand Popsicles."

And then she was praying. "Dear Daddy Stan, I love you. I wish that you didn't die. Amen."

When Heidi took my hand to walk back to the car, I knew that I'd become her dad, that Stan would always be her father, and that there was room for both of us in our family. On a selfish level, I needed to keep Stan in his daughter's heart. I knew it would be good for her. But keeping such a link intact would also set well with the many other people who loved this little girl. I wanted them to know I embraced the responsibility.

In effect, I made a silent pact with Stan that day to take

---

care of his daughter—if for no other reason than that his daughter had come to expect it of me.

— • —

Perhaps that's why I was so intrigued, and maybe a bit confused, by Sara Pogue's ideas about family, and fatherhood in particular. A twenty-two-year-old Washington State University student, Sara had a five-month-old son named Xavier. They lived in a small apartment complex on the WSU campus.

"I think our society is so hung up on what should be. They have everything so black and white," said Sara. "There has to be a mother, father, and child. But I don't think that's necessary."

Sara challenged traditional family concepts. In fact, when I interviewed her, she all but announced that she and her son were helping redefine the American family. A full-time student and volunteer for a number of sexual awareness groups, Sara said she'd tried to practice what she preached about being sexually active but had accidentally gotten pregnant. And, according to Sara, Xavier's father was out of the picture.

I asked if they'd ever want to get back together, maybe get married and be a family.

"This isn't where I would have wanted to be," Sara conceded. "But one of the things about Xavier coming into my life is, I had to snap together right away. . . . It's not such a bad thing. I mean, I was an anthropology major and studied parenting styles. Children need equal time with both sexes, but it doesn't have to be a mother and a father.

"We're really moving as a society away from a two-parent household. So by the time Xavier is old enough to realize he doesn't have a father, many of his classmates won't either."

I was stunned. The thought of fatherless families by design had me raising my eyebrows. But I couldn't judge Sara. She was simply struggling to find a place for her and her son in a society where family had become a matter of debate instead of definition. How had this come to be? I thought about the portrait of my parents that rests atop the old upright piano in the living room of our log house. The black-and-white picture was taken in the late 1930s. Dad is tall, slender, handsome, and decked out in white shoes. Mom is wearing a ribbon in her hair and a flowered dress that flatters her figure. There's an aura of courtship about them.

I often take the picture down, wipe the dust from the glass with the cuff of my sleeve, and simply stare through the window. I like the photograph because it hints of our family and reminds me that Dad and I had unfinished business.

My father, Roy, was an intensely devoted family man. He was obsessively precise and tried to keep everything from his dresser drawer to his fishing tackle box in perfect order. He did his work for the SooLine Railroad the same way. I was always impressed with how businesslike he kept his desk and office. He liked his cars washed, the lawn mowed, dinner on time, and his kids dressed properly. He never spanked me and rarely offered a hug. I think he hugged my little sister a lot. Dad taught me to shake hands, firmly, like a man. Come to think of it, my older brother and I have never hugged. We shake hands, firmly, like men.

Not once did Dad play catch, shoot a basket, or throw a football with me. Yet he was there with Mom at all my high school games. We went fishing a lot and he took my brother and me to the stock car races. Sometimes, when he got in a surly mood, I was glad when work took him out of town. But I never heard anyone outside the family say a bad thing about him.

One day in late May of 1972, my dad ran to catch a bus for work, boarded it, and collapsed in the aisle from a massive heart attack. He never regained consciousness and died two weeks later, just six months after I moved away from our home in Minnesota to Idaho. He was fifty-five. Mom never remarried. And I never got to tell my dad that I really loved him—and that I knew he really loved me.

With all that in mind, I talked again to Sara about a year later while doing research on a story about family values in connection with a political campaign. She was doing laundry when I called. Xavier was sleeping. His father was still out of the picture.

"Xavier's dad has never seen him and as far as I know he doesn't want to see him," said Sara.

I couldn't imagine not wanting to see your own child.

In his first year, Xavier had learned to walk. He'd also suffered through ear infections and was late to start talking because of the ailments. But he'd made up for lost time, said Sara.

"He says 'water' and 'thank you' and he says 'Ashley' a lot, which is the name of my parents' dog."

Sara hoped to graduate soon and had taken a new job. She was working full-time as a cook. Xavier went to day care.

"It's not what I consider the ideal situation," said Sara, "but it's working out quite well. I don't think it makes a difference that Xavier doesn't have a father. Because my family loves him," said Sara. "And you know, he doesn't really know the difference."

— • —

Heidi and Greta never had a doubt about the roles their parents played. They had a go-to-work dad and a stay-at-home mom. With Diane especially, the girls expected nothing else.

In a way, Diane and Heidi faced a fate similar to Sara Pogue and little Xavier's. And like Sara, I'm sure Diane would have made the best of being a single parent.

"But I don't want to be alone," Diane told me early in our relationship. "I want to have a family. I'm a homebody. I don't want to go to work and leave Heidi with someone else."

"We're lucky we found each other," I said. "I'm your man." In fact, I considered myself the most fortunate man in the world to have found a new love through my work, of all things. But it took me a bit longer to appreciate how much I benefited from Diane's desire to tend the domestic front.

Even when I returned from work to a warm house full of dinner smells, I didn't "get it" for a long time. As a matter of routine, we'd eat and I'd play with the girls before pounding out a story or two for the newspaper. Then, at bedtime, I'd listen to prayers, maybe sing a verse of "The Bear Went Over the Mountain," return downstairs, and find Diane spent.

"I'm really beat," she'd almost apologize, slumping into my arms. "I'll go up and finish tucking them in." The girls seemed to demand a final maternal touch before drifting off to sleep; a peck on the cheek from Dad was wanted, but a hug from Mom was absolutely necessary.

So I began to ponder my wife's position in our family. Nothing, after all, spoke more to a redefinition of family in our society over the past four decades than the evolution of a woman's place in the home. By the mid-1980s, Diane had become a stay-at-home exception. Working moms, like Denise Stanzak, were the norm.

Denise, in fact, was just the second person to be featured in my column and she confided that sometimes she was at her wits' end.

"I need a change of pace," she said when I called and asked for an interview. "Sure, why not? I'll do it."

Already harried by a day's work at the hospital when I arrived at her home, Denise had stripped her fifteen-month-old son down to his diaper, propped him in his high chair, and was preparing for a mess.

The family springer spaniels, Duke and Duchess, took up their accustomed stations within licking distance of young Nickolas's dangling feet. It was spaghetti time.

"Life was so uncomplicated when I was single," Denise said as Nickolas painted his face with one hand and used a spoon to stir his supper with the other hand. Duke, eyes locked on the spoon draped in noodles and sauce, made a quick swipe with his tongue and went motionless.

"Yaaaa," Nickolas squealed, using his free hand to scoop a fistful out of the bowl and launch it onto the floor. Duke peeled out across the linoleum, beat Duchess to the appetizer, slurped it up, and returned to his station.

Nickolas smiled at my attention, let out another squeal, and crushed an even bigger wad of spaghetti on his forehead. I apologized for encouraging him.

"That's all right," Denise said while using a damp cloth to wipe her son's entire head clean again. "I'm used to this." Nickolas grinned through a mouthful of spaghetti. Just prior to my arrival, he'd pulled a pot of water off the kitchen counter.

Denise and her husband, Joseph, lived with Nickolas and the family dogs in Uniontown, Washington. The farming community was settled in the late 1880s by German immigrants and is still home for Saint Boniface Catholic Church, the oldest Catholic church in the state. Joseph was nearing the end of his paper chase some fifteen miles across the border at the University of Idaho College of Law.

"Finals time is right now. Everything is getting real tense," said Denise, as if she herself would be taking the battery of tests.

Like so many hamlets surrounding the university towns of Moscow and Pullman, Uniontown was known as a bedroom community. Snuggled in a blanket of rolling wheat fields, it offered a temporary home for young families like the Stanzaks caught amid the push and pull of making ends meet.

I sympathized with Denise. Even though the insurance money got us started, we always seemed strapped. Between seeing to the girls' needs, the land mortgage, the cost of continued house construction, buying groceries, and tending to all the animals that seemed never to stop accumulating, my salary was all but spent before I cashed the payroll checks.

"Things are always more involved than you expect," Denise agreed about family life. A registered nurse, she worked four days a week as a supervisor on the second floor of Moscow's Gritman Memorial Hospital. Back home, she cared for Nickolas. She was also three months pregnant.

I couldn't grasp how she handled it all.

"Well, on my days off, I clean the house and do laundry . . . and . . ."

About the time Denise was explaining how to cram ten days of responsibilities into one week and Nickolas was nearing the bottom of his spaghetti bowl, Joseph drove up. A brawny guy who looked more like a logger than a lawyer, he shook my hand and I explained why I was in the kitchen with his wife.

"She's a godsend," volunteered Joseph, sitting down at the table with me. "That's all I can say."

I wrote his words in my notebook, underlined "godsend," and thought about Diane. I could see her at home with the girls, maybe refereeing a squabble, preparing dinner, washing dishes, or doing laundry.

"I hate to interrupt," interrupted Denise, "but I've got to put some clothes on him." She scooped her spaghetti-slathered son from his high chair and headed for his bedroom. Joseph watched them leave, inched his chair closer to me, and leaned over, the way guys do when they share a secret that's not really a secret.

"To show you how hard it's been for Denise," he tried to whisper, "she's been in the hospital sick once every semester."

"I think I get run down and catch what's in the hospital," said Denise from somewhere down the hallway, proving once again that women are better listeners than men are whisperers. I told him he was lucky.

He nodded, the way guys do when they really, really know how lucky they are. Denise, he said, made much more than money.

"She makes the family work."

I went home that night to hugs and kisses and a house filled with those familiar dinner smells.

"Hi, hon," Diane greeted me. "Come on, girls. Dad's home. It's time to eat."

I can't remember what we ate that night. The table talk also escapes me. But it was somewhere back then, after coming home day after day from my supposed "real job," that I began to understand my wife's take on family. She saw it as a true labor of love. Her dedication to her job was written in the lines on her face—especially when her "day at the office" hadn't gone well, everything seemed to be in disarray, and nothing would happen on time.

"Sometimes, David, I think maybe you're bored with me. Remember when we got married, I warned you I was a homebody and I worried you might resent my keeping you from your career, going to a bigger newspaper and—"

"That's not true," I retorted.

"Well, sometimes I feel that way," said Diane. "I think we just need to appreciate each other a little better. That's what families do."

"You're right."

"The most important thing for me, David, is to be Heidi and Greta's mom."

"I appreciate that."

"I hope so. I really hope so. Somebody has to make this family work, and I don't think it's a one-person job."

"You're right. You're so right," I relented. "I understand. I'll try to do a better job from my end."

"I hope so." Diane sighed, the hint of a smile betraying her stern demeanor.

"I'll do better."

— • —

I've decided that my attraction to family life stems from growing up in a place where every family was nuclear and every home provided an extra catcher or right fielder or shortstop. It's that simple. As Minneapolis suburbs go, Fridley in the 1950s was a fresh face on the northern horizon and Hillcrest Drive was a *Wonder Years* kind of neighborhood.

We had enough kids to field sandlot baseball teams all summer long. Lush green lawns blended from one yard to the next, the smell of barbecue filled the air on weekends, and huge oak trees made climbing to new heights easy for my friends and me. Come winter, Hillcrest Drive became a downhill dragstrip for our Flexible Flyers, and blizzards were followed by weather cold enough to shatter hockey pucks.

The kids in my neighborhood grew up with the Minnesota Twins franchise. We played game after game and wore Twins hats through the sweltering days of June, July, and August until the sweatbands rotted out.

I don't know if life was better or worse in the world of sandlot baseball and street games, but everyone just seemed more secure in their roles, for better or for worse.

For instance, I could never imagine saying a girl played better baseball than me, even though I'm old enough now to admit that a couple of the best players were Kathy Knudson and Christine Kirch. In the clutch, the two girls could throw, catch, bat, and run with most of us boys. Come game day for the local Braves Little League team, however, and they got relegated to the bleachers.

And yet Fate was kind enough to grant me two daughters who had the opportunity, along with their girlfriends, to show that athletics contained a void only women could fill. I realize now that "throwing like a girl" can be a *compliment*, even to nine-year-old boys.

Tyson Thorton and Lucas McIntosh were nine-year-old best friends when one of them answered my call from the *Tribune* and we arranged to meet at the ballpark. I could see myself in their eyes. Things hadn't changed when it came time to "play ball." They were dreamers like I was. The two had only a few days of school left before they resumed their pursuit of the big leagues. Just talking with them was like donning that sweaty old Twins hat again and stepping back into childhood.

Tyson was a shortstop and Lucas was a catcher for the

Weippe Dodgers. The boys played in an intermediate base-ball league where, according to Tyson and Lucas, a me-chanical pitching machine threw strikes right down the middle.

"We use hardballs, not softballs," said Tyson, swinging a phantom bat and pretending to go downtown.

So who's the best player? I queried.

"Lindsay is a good baseball player," conceded Tyson.

"And basketball too," added Lucas. "She's really a good basketball player."

She. She's a good baseball player. Yikes.

Lindsay Hartig was the daughter of the Weippe Dodgers' coach. And the boys seemed a bit befuddled if not by Lind-say's presence on the team, then by her prowess.

"Sometimes girls are nice," said Lucas, shrugging his shoulders as if he wanted to change the subject, "and some-times, well, you know."

Both Tyson and Lucas were fans of the major leagues. Lucas liked the Chicago Cubs and Tyson leaned toward San Francisco. They really wanted to be Seattle Mariners fans, if they could ever go to a game. But kids living in re-mote Idaho, they said, pretty much have to depend on tele-vision to see the real heroes of baseball play the game.

Then again, Tyson and Lucas said, the chances that they themselves might play in the "Bigs" someday were "pretty good." After all, they were about to make front-page news. And the season hadn't even started.

"Wait 'til Lindsay sees us!"

"Yeah!"

I suddenly regretted taking Kathy and Christine for granted.

— • —

More than anything, Diane and I wanted Heidi and Greta to cherish their childhood and embrace the memories when they got older. Greta had no problem. From the beginning, she was enamored by country life to the point of being fearless about things like the woods, the dark, and even coyotes howling in our backyard.

"I see a moon," she piped up every time we went outside on a moonlit night. She loved to explore and poke around in the dirt, and find things under rocks. Sometimes she asked Mom to wash her hands because when she sucked her thumb it tasted "like a centipede."

Heidi, on the other hand, was like the little bear we sang about that "went over the mountain." She was fascinated by the lights of Moscow beckoning in the night and even bigger cities awaiting her arrival beyond. Like her sister, she grew up riding horses, swimming in the pond, participating in 4-H, and otherwise relishing a pretty carefree childhood. But sometimes rural life seemed to get the best of her and she'd ask questions like "Why do we have to cut firewood? Why can't we just have a furnace with a thermostat?"

"Life is not a thermostat, it's a woodpile," I'd tell Heidi.

"Yeah, I know," she'd humor me. "And there's no such thing as a free lunch."

By the time Heidi was in high school, our disagreements began to threaten the family. She'd grown from that little toddler who tumbled into my camera bag to a teenager who seemingly spent much of her senior year disengaging from the family, especially from me. In retrospect, it wasn't anything all that serious. But I didn't like her behavior. And sometimes we'd end up reminding each other that we didn't share blood.

One morning before leaving for school, Heidi suggested

that it was time for her to move out rather than listen to my ranting.

"Stop making threats unless you plan to live up to them," I said.

I came home that night to a distraught wife who informed me that our daughter hadn't come home. She was staying at a friend's house. It was Christmastime and suddenly there was nothing merry about the season.

"What did you say to her?" Diane implored.

"I guess I told her to put up or shut up," I said.

Heidi stayed away for three days. We knew of her every movement because the friend's parents were as worried as Diane and I. They took Heidi into their home until she was ready to return to ours. When she did come home, not much was said. I really don't remember anything about that Christmas, other than that I'd failed as a father by driving our daughter away from the people who loved her most.

And then my column steered me to Bob and Clara Davaz, who provided some perspective. They offered their ideas on family and parenting by telling stories of troubled children who came into their home. The Davazes were foster parents. And both concurred that the typical American family had become riven by discord. Evidence of such strife was everywhere, said Bob and Clara, even in the remote town of Ahsahka, Idaho. So they weren't surprised to hear my tale of woe.

Owners of the Woodlot Tavern and Café, Bob, sixty-three, and Clara, sixty-two, lived and worked near the base of towering Dworshak Dam. At 717 feet tall and 3,000 feet long, Dworshak clogs the North Fork of the Clearwater River and is one of the largest dams in the country.

The trapped waters of the North Fork spill incessantly from the front of the dam, settle into a pool, and take a languid journey for about half a mile along the eastern edge of

Ahsahka before emptying into the main stem of the Clear-water River. The afternoon of my arrival was cold, and the Davazes fueled the conversation with hot coffee and stories that struck close to home.

"We were the only ones who took teenage girls," Clara said, her words making me think of my own daughters, especially Heidi. "There were a lot of mirrors in the house."

Bob and Clara looked unassuming but talked with authority. The Idaho Department of Health and Welfare had recognized them as Foster Parents of the Year. The two had also raised five children of their own and boasted of four-teen grandchildren and five great-grandchildren.

"There's always a need for good foster homes," said Clara.

Where did all the kids come from?

"Everywhere," said Bob and Clara in unison.

"Most of the kids had trouble communicating with their parents," said Bob, "or they were abused."

"And it seemed like every time they [the authorities] got a teenager down here, they'd come to us to give the kid a place to stay," said Clara.

At one time, the Davazes had six girls living in their home, along with their own children.

"When we had all those girls," Clara said with a big sigh, "I spent a lot of nights on the weekends at two or three o'clock in the morning looking for them." She told about finding a runaway in the Clearwater County Jail one night. "I left that girl in jail for twenty-three hours and fifty-nine minutes—one minute shy of the maximum the police would hold her—and that cured everything."

I sense that Clara and Bob were practicing proverbial "tough love" long before it became fashionable. Some-times, said Bob, consequences are the only things a teen can understand.

"I laid the law down to them," he growled. "I let them know the door swung two ways."

I pondered Bob's words. It had been just a year since I'd tried to administer my own measure of tough love with Heidi and failed.

"There's still time," Clara assured. Youngsters, she and Bob insisted, need and actually want boundaries. They also need, but may not want, adults to help keep them within those boundaries.

"The main thing was, if they had a question, they knew they could ask us," Clara said of the way she dealt with her own youngsters and the foster children.

That's it, I thought. That's why I'd failed with Heidi. She hardly wanted to talk, let alone confide in me. But how, I wondered, could Bob and Clara give so much of themselves to so many kids? Why?

Bob and Clara looked at each other, then at me like I was a bit daft. The question had apparently never crossed their minds.

"You have to," Bob finally declared, "for the love of the kids."

Clara nodded agreement.

What other reason could there be for the Davazes to take so many children into their home? It surely wasn't for the meager stipend the state paid to foster parents, or for the award they won.

I sit here now pondering the old adage "There but for the grace of God go I." There, I now realize, but for the love of parents go our children. I'd almost blown it with Heidi. Rather than define the boundaries in her teenage life, I'd unwittingly pushed her beyond them with a misapplied form of tough love. Luckily, she was as tough as she was petulant. She came back and, since the experience, I can only hope we've both grown wiser and closer.

———

"Dear Mom and Dad," wrote Heidi, who is now twenty-three and living in Boise, in a recent Valentine card. "There's no such thing as a free lunch. Thanks for never bailing me out. Thanks for not letting me think life would be easy. It's hard, but it's beautiful and I appreciate it so much. It's the greatest gift you could have ever given me."

"Dear Heidi," I e-mailed her back. "Thanks for the Valentine stuff and the card. Don't tell anybody, but you are my greatest gift. Without you, I wouldn't have met your mom. Without your mom, there wouldn't have been a Greta. And without all three of you girls, I wouldn't have a family. Come home and visit soon. Lunch is on me. Love, Dad."

— • —

Irony can be such a sweet and gentle teacher. While I struggled with Heidi during her teenage years and worried that our family might unravel, a couple of teenagers helped me understand what keeps a family together.

"That's when we got married," said Eric Engle, proudly showing me a framed photograph of him and his wife, Kim, when I arrived to interview them. The photo was taken shortly after their wedding in Honeyville, Utah.

At the time, Eric was fifteen and Kim was just two years older.

"We had a justice of the peace marry us. He knew exactly what we went down there for," Eric said.

Kim was pregnant. "We loved each other," she explained.

By the time I met the Engles, the wedding picture was more than four years old and Kim and Eric were already beating the odds. Teenage marriages just aren't supposed to work. But their bond, insisted Eric and Kim, had grown stronger.

"I guess we were kind of young," conceded Eric.

After the wedding, the Engles returned to Orofino. Their daughter, Kelsey Jo, was born and Eric remained in high school for two years. Kim, who graduated with honors from high school, attended Valley Business College at Lewiston.

"My friends didn't really even want to be around me when I got married," said Eric. He eventually lost touch with most of them and dropped out of school. Everyone seemed to be waiting for the marriage to fall apart—everyone except Eric and Kim.

"We like being married," said Kim.

"If you stay together and combine your energy, you can make it," said Eric.

"It took a lot of growing up," added Kim.

The family had also grown. In addition to Kelsey Jo, who was four, there was one-year-old Jeremy. Hoping to give his family a chance for an even better future, Eric, a member of the Army National Guard, had signed up for a hitch with the regular army as a combat engineer.

"I drive a five-ton dump truck," said Eric. "We're the ones who go out before the infantry and build bridges and roads so they can cross."

Like a lot of young service families in the mid-to-late 1980s, the Engles considered the military an opportunity.

"Oh, I'm happy. We'll get away for a while," said Kim, anticipating the move to Fort Lewis, near Olympia, Washington.

"Away for a while?" mused Eric. "It's going to be four years."

Then I popped the question.

"What's the secret? What continues to keep your family together?"

"Love," said Kim without hesitation.

Just love? I thought. The word seemed to give short shrift to all the ingredients needed to keep intact a family built from a teenage marriage.

"I think it's love too," said Eric. "We've been through a lot."

"So," I said, pausing to make sure my final question didn't smack of too much insensitivity, "if you had to make the same decision, knowing everything you know today, would you have still ended up in Honeyville?"

"Yes," said Kim, smiling broadly and pulling Kelsey Jo and Jeremy closer.

"We both love each other," Eric said, as if he might need to pound the thought into my head. "I could have been just like any other guy and said, 'Hey, it's not my kid.' But that wouldn't have been right."

The Engles' story appeared on the front page of the *Tribune* and triggered a flurry of bets in the newsroom about whether they'd really make it. The couple eventually made the military move to Olympia shortly afterward and Eric became a member of the 101st Airborne, serving in Iraq during Desert Storm.

By the time I recontacted them in the summer of 1994, the family, still growing, had come full circle back to the same house where we first talked.

"We're still together. It's been eleven years," said Eric matter-of-factly.

Eric was still driving a truck for a living. Kim was home with not just Kelsey Jo, who was now eleven, and Jeremy, eight, but also with three-year-old Kayla and one-year-old Ryan.

"We stuck it out," said Eric.

I talked again with Eric in 1998 and asked if he and Kim and the kids could define the concept of family. I encouraged them to put something on paper.

Kelsey Jo, who'd grown to fourteen years old, answered the phone the next night and said she had the definition in hand.

"We all agreed on this, even the little kids. Do you want me to read it?"

She seemed delighted.

"Sure," I said, eager to hear what they'd come up with.

The entire family, said Kelsey Jo, sat down around the kitchen table and took about ten minutes to compose the following:

> A family is the people who will love and be there for you no matter what. They are there to pick you up in hard times and to share your joy. You never give up on them and you'll do whatever it takes to stay together; such as compromise, communicate, sacrifice and most of all, love one another. A family is your heart and soul next to God.

I don't know that a better portrait could be painted.

— • —

I recently convinced my mother, Marjorie, to sit down in front of our video camera and reminisce about her life. I felt a sense of urgency. Not that Mom, who was eighty-one years old at the time, was failing. On the contrary, she welcomed the request as yet another new experience to fill her day. She seemed pleasantly pleased that her son, the one who had left home, had come back with a burning interest in what remained of his family.

"Just start at the beginning, Mom. Tell me about your first memories," I instructed. We spent the better part of two hours together, touching on the highlights of her childhood, meeting Dad, their marriage, the joy and demands of raising three children, and the wonders of looking back at it all like it was just yesterday. I already cherish the videotape.

"I think I've had a good life," said Mom toward the end of our session. "And I've had some pretty bad bumps."

"How do you get through those?"

"I pray. And I'm sure there's a hereafter. The only thing is when I go, I don't want my kids or grandchildren crying about me. I've had a good life and I'm ready."

"So what do you want to say finally on this tape?"

"That I love you all."

"And we love you."

"I'd like to see you all do the best you can in life and be good to everybody else. And don't forget each other. I think of other families who don't speak and I think it's so sad. And I don't want to see that happen with my family."

Sitting there with my mother, I was suddenly a fifty-two-year-old boy. I was the kid again, listening to the wisdom of a parent and wishing I'd heeded more of her words, and those of my dad, when I was younger. How fortunate to have Mom around to confirm just how important family really is.

— • —

My wife watches the video with mixed emotions. She adores my mother. And she shares all those warm feelings about family. But I've never known Diane to reminisce with her own mother in the same way.

"It's really hard," she told me shortly after we met in

1977 and I started asking about her mother's peculiar ways. Alice seemed obsessed with her children. The nest was empty, but she still considered them under her wing. She kept lists of things to do and read them over the phone to Diane. She rattled around in her house all alone and sometimes sat wrapped in her own arms while rocking back and forth on the edge of a chair. Now and then she'd make awkward movements with her arms and hands.

"Mama can't help it," Diane would insist. "She can't help the way she is."

But I wouldn't buy that explanation.

"Oh come on," I'd try to challenge Diane. "Don't you think a lot of your mother's problems are her own doing? She just needs to get out and do things. She's too involved with her children. She misses you too much. You kids are all grown up now. You've got lives of your own. And your dad isn't with her. She needs to strike out on her own a little."

"Her family has always been the most important thing in her life," said Diane. "She can't just change that. And she's mentally sick. You know that, David. But I wonder if you accept that."

I didn't accept it. Moreover, I wouldn't accept Diane's bigger concern: that she would someday suffer like her mother from loneliness and what I considered self-inflicted torment.

"Don't worry about that," I tried to console Diane. "I won't let that happen to you. And you won't let it happen. You've seen how hard it is, not just for your mother, but for you and everyone else."

"I know. But I dread what the future might hold."

"The future will be good, whatever you make of it. We come from good families and have a good family of our own. What could get in the way of that?"

CHAPTER FIVE

Reaping a Lifestyle

Tractor triage is something real farmers do without think-ing. They can probe the innards of an internal combustion engine and readily discern whether any life is left. But I'm not a real farmer. I know little or nothing about things me-chanical, especially tractors. So when it came time for the resurrection of Allis, my best tool was a prayer of frustra-tion.

Allis, as in the Allis Chalmers Tractor Company, goes way back to when Diane and I got married. We bought the old orange tractor from friends near Deary, Idaho, and drove her home some twenty miles on a country road. The trip took about two hours. Allis came with a belly-mounted sickle for mowing hay, but had no other implements such as a plow, disc, or harrow. She boasted only twenty-five horsepower and for that reason alone wasn't the kind of tractor to use on a real farm.

But like I said, I wasn't a real farmer. And besides, Diane liked Allis from the get-go. She talked to her all the way home as we shared the seat and took turns driving.

"Just keep going, girl. Not too much farther."

Over the years, the little tractor became a partner in our modest attempts to live close to the land. We hauled hay and wood with Allis, harrowed the horse pasture with a section of chain-link fence, and pulled kids around in a trailer when it came time for birthday parties.

But as with all things mechanical and neglected, Allis eventually stopped running. She went into a deep coma and even my prayers of frustration failed to resuscitate her. Tall grass grew up and all but consumed Allis's hulk. Sitting all alone in the pasture, she began to look like one of those still-life photographs in magazines that try to capture the charm of country living.

"David, how come Allis doesn't run?" Diane finally asked.

It's at times like this that I wonder if Diane might have been better off with a farm boy, rather than a city kid, for a husband.

"Well, what are you going to do, just let her sit there? We can use her around here and . . ."

So I crawled into my farmer coveralls, pulled on my boots, and ventured out to where Allis sat oxidizing in the September sun. Life fluids, I thought. Were there any left? I checked the radiator and found some gunky antifreeze that appeared still to be in liquid form. Next, pull the oil dipstick. About half a quart low. Finally, peer into the fuel tank. Empty.

Come to think of it, the last vital sign to stop when Allis succumbed was a steady drip, drip, drip that leaked from around something called the sediment bowl. The bowl hangs just under the gasoline tank and, I was told later by a real tractor mechanic, has the job of filtering the equivalent of engine cholesterol from the gas tank before it gets to the carburetor and plugs an artery.

It took me an entire day to remove, clean, and replace the sediment bowl, the gasoline tank, and the rest of the fuel line. I'd never done anything like this before. A new sediment bowl, battery, oil, and filter plus a shot of additional antifreeze set me back about sixty dollars. The following day, I returned to the pasture with a gallon of regular gasoline and gave Allis her first drink in more than a year. She swallowed and I swear I heard a belch.

I climbed aboard, sat down in the seat, set the throttle, pulled the choke, depressed the starter, and began to pray.

Allis groaned like her digestive tract had rusted together.

I let off the starter, took a deep breath, and gave it another try.

Kajunk, kajunk, kajunk . . . kaBaaaaam!

The soup can I'd used to cap Allis's upright exhaust pipe and protect her innards from the rain blasted into the air like a rocket, landing about twenty feet away. Allis roared like a teenager being awakened before noon on Saturday. Black, then blue, then white smoke billowed from her exhaust pipe.

"She's alive!"

I jumped down and stood back, my arms spread wide in worship, while the plume of smoke rose from Allis toward the heavens and she evacuated her craw of all that had collected there over the months.

"She's alive!"

At the sound of Allis's sprightly roar, Diane came out the front door of our house and stood applauding her farmer husband. I danced in the grass, patted Allis's sides, kicked her tires, and reached over to pull back the throttle. She idled obediently as I walked around her looking for leaks, more smoke, fire, or anything else that might indicate doom. The little orange tractor had returned from the dead.

"Welcome back, Allis."

I suddenly felt like plowing a field.

— • —

Allis has come to symbolize our life here on Hatter Creek: nostalgic, temperamental, rewarding, and always in need of maintenance. She's become a barometer of sorts, a gauge that reflects our well-being. When Allis is running, it means I've taken the necessary time to shore up the home front. When the little tractor refuses to start, it usually means my priorities are the wrong ones.

With some luck, a few prayers, and about ten gallons of gasoline, I could probably pilot Allis to the top of Moscow Mountain, look back at our house and then west toward real farm country. From the mile-high vantage, Idaho's forests fade quickly into fingers of trees that reach out and caress the rich soils of the Palouse Country at the southeastern edge of Washington State. It is a magical zone of transition where stands of pine, fir, tamarack, and cedar give way to fields of wheat, barley, peas, and lentils. Breaking out of the forest, the land seems to stretch forever toward the Pacific Ocean.

Since the day more than twenty-five years ago when I decided to call this place home, the question has always been "How do I fit in here?" How am I supposed to be a farmer when my training is in newspaper reporting?

"We don't have to be farmers," Diane has always insisted. "Not like living off the land . . . we can be *part* of the land." Sometime after we moved in, she said, "Look at the old cabin down there. Alec Bull and his wife built it all those years ago and it seems so lonely now. We can finish what they started. We can become part of this place. A lot of people would come up here and maybe move into a mobile home and call it good. I want us to fit into the landscape. I don't want to detract from it. I want us to be part of the ebb and flow of this country."

At times, the Palouse can indeed take on a spellbinding, sea-like appearance. The rolling countryside was created millions of years ago by the laggardly advance and retreat of glaciers, followed by the centuries-long deposit of wind-blown soil and volcanic ash. Over the ages, a deep, rich loess accumulated and the region became awash in waves of prairie grass. Today, the scene continues to move from one season to the next. People who work the ground have learned to bend not only with the forces of nature, but to the fickle fluctuations of the agriculture economy.

I love to hear about the old days and look at historical pictures. The yesteryear people seemed so in tune with their environment and focused on the work at hand. Most of the heavy chores, of course, were done with horses. Hitches of twenty to thirty Belgian or Percheron drafts leaned into the harnesses and pulled the ferrous imple-ments needed to till the land and harvest the crops. The growing seasons revolved around a horn of plenty and a lifestyle that was upright and profitable. If I squint into the sunset from atop the mountain, I can almost revisit the scene.

At least that's my romantic conception of it all. And I think Diane would agree.

— • —

Phil Largent, on the other hand, was familiar enough with farming's past to know he couldn't bank on the future, and surely not on romance. Yet he was singing in the rain when I drove into his driveway one spring day and accepted an invitation to sit down for a cup of black coffee and a shot of good news. It was, in fact, raining again at the right place, the right time, and in the right amount. Phil looked out the window of his farmhouse, all but crossed his fingers, and made a prediction.

"Potentially, I've never seen it look so good."

Phil was a fifty-nine-year-old third-generation wheat farmer who worked ground about fifteen miles southwest of Colfax, Washington, out where agriculture literally envelops the countryside. Immediately on shaking his hand, I knew we came from different worlds. Not only was his tractor much bigger than mine, but Phil had literally invested his life in the land.

"I see a year where we could have real storage problems come harvest," he said. "Wheat piled everywhere."

Growing crops has never been much of a problem in the rich Palouse region. The farms date back a century or more, and much of agriculture technology's leading edge has been honed here. After horses gave way to tractors, bigger and bigger machines became the norm. Tractors with up to twelve drive wheels and self-leveling combines have negotiated the undulating terrain for the better part of three decades.

As Phil and I talked on this day in early June, farmers throughout the Palouse were easing into the traditional lull before the combines hit the fields. The weather dictated the immediate future. Drought-quenching rain fell throughout May, and with it came talk of big yields everywhere.

"When things are going good, harvest can be . . . well, there's a little excitement," said Phil.

The rain gauges nailed to a fence post outside Phil's house told the story. Since the first of January, about two inches had fallen. That's a lot less than some places, said Phil, but well above normal for this part of the country. Green crops signaled good fortune.

Of course, farming can be bittersweet work that hinges

not just on toil, determination, and economic markets, but also on the whims of nature. All the excitement, Phil explained, could change to gloom if disease, hail, or some other disaster took its toll. So those who tilled the ground held their breath as they looked for the skies to clear, temperatures to rise, and the crops to mature.

Besides, said Phil, when it came to farming, one good year couldn't lead to prosperity, even though one bad year could spell disaster. "Certainly the eighties were difficult . . . challenging, we should say, compared to the thirties." He pointed out that there'd been two generations of "unprecedented prosperity" from the 1930s until the late 1970s.

"People developed certain bad habits. No matter what you paid for land, it was worth more five years later. That wasn't true in the eighties." And those farmers who were too heavily "leveraged" with borrowed money paid a price. Many went under. What remained, said Phil, was an agriculture industry that had to tighten its financial belt several notches at a time.

"We had cheap money for so many years. Now I think a person will have to be more of a fiscal conservative."

I'd heard the same kind of talk for years while searching the farm country for news. Sometimes I stopped in places like the town of Palouse, Washington, where on rainy days a gaggle of farmers usually hung out in one of the town's two "whineries." The whineries were restaurants where the men met in the morning over cups of coffee to whine about the weather, the price of grain, and such. I heard one of my first wheat-farmer jokes at such a gathering. Somebody asked why dead farmers get buried only one foot deep. Everybody shrugged.

"So they can always get their handout."

I thought it was pretty darn funny. But most of the men

seemed only mildly amused. Farmers everywhere find little humor in their struggles with government programs that, while extending a measure of financial security, dictate how they go about their business. Federal "handouts" come with a lot of strings attached.

"Profit margins are tighter," Phil said, explaining that worldwide competition was getting fiercer. "You'd like to think the world operated on a free-market basis, but it doesn't. There are so many hungry people in the world, but they don't have the money to pay for it."

Phil lived with his wife, Josie, in the old Long Hollow Schoolhouse that the two had converted into a spacious modern home. As a boy, Phil attended classes in the school. He was currently farming with his son and one of his brothers. Farming itself, said Phil, had become more about balance-sheet management than the actual sowing and harvesting of crops.

"Politics governs it all," said Phil. And politics are harder to predict than wheat prices. In fact, the price of wheat had fallen more than a dollar a bushel in six months. The trend had little to do with demand but everything to do with politics, he said. And as for how the price might be kicked higher, Phil could only say, "I wish I had the smarts to answer that." The only thing he and other farmers could do was keep one eye on the rain gauge and the other on the promise of a good harvest.

Most days I drive through farm country without a second thought about people like Phil. I watch the fields green up in the spring, the crops ripen in the summer, the bounty harvested in the fall, and the landscape blanketed white with the first snows of winter. It all happens with such pre-dictability that I sometimes lose sight of the dynamics at work and the changes that continue to take place in the nation's farm country—changes that have had an impact even on our small acreage.

— • —

When I was a kid living in the suburbs of Minneapolis, our family used to get in the Chevrolet once or twice a year and drive to Wisconsin, where my mother's uncle Fred owned a real live dairy farm, the kind of place Diane would have loved.

"I really was born decades too late," she lamented one morning at breakfast while we talked about our "farm" and how hard it would be to actually start farming. "When I think of a farm, it's the old farms with cows and chickens and maybe some pasture and a field with corn or wheat. And a big old barn."

"And kittens in the haymow."

"Yeah. And maybe a pig or two . . . and a big kitchen with a big heavy table everybody could sit around."

My wife's dream seemed to mirror my memories of waking up early in the morning at Uncle Fred's farm to watch the cows get milked. Afterward, I'd return with the men to a kitchen filled with breakfast smells and farmer talk.

"We'd sit around the table and Aunt Emily, she was always there wearing her apron."

Diane smiled at the image as she busied herself over the stove. My wife reminded me not only of Aunt Emily, but of other "farmwives" I'd met while doing my column. Even though farms are much larger and less diversified today, the farm kitchen still offers some special insight into what it means to "work the land." If you want to know "the secret recipe" of successful farming, you need look no further than the domains of women like Aunt Emily and Katherine Zenner.

"My husband is seventy-three and he's out driving a tractor right now," Katherine announced when I pulled a chair
up to her kitchen table. "You'll have to wait to talk to
him."

I protested that we'd agreed to do a story about her, but
the words were lost amid the clatter of kitchen work.
Katherine was baking cookies.

"Chocolate chip," she announced while taking out one
batch, putting in another, and setting the timer on the
oven.

Spring had arrived. The countryside around Genesee,
Idaho, growled with the sound of tractors. Farmers like
Katherine's husband were in the fields planting. Farmwives, like Katherine, were more likely in the kitchen.
Farm women, both young and old, have an old-fashioned
pride about their positions. Most like being called
farmwives. There's no denying such a title when they marry
a farmer. But they also know what goes into the job description behind the title.

"We had to make chicken fly through the broth that
day," said Katherine, recalling a time when six unannounced farmhands approached the house with hunger
written on their faces.

A buzzer on the stove interrupted her story.

"That's my cookies. Excuse me . . . they aren't burning
yet."

I watched her move as efficiently as her husband tilled
his fields. She slipped her hands into oven mittens, pulled
down the oven door with the right hand, snatched the
batch of baked cookies with the left, set them on a trivet,
swooped up another fresh batch, reloaded the oven, closed
the door, set aside the gloves, and returned to our conversation.

"There's always a story brewing on the farm this time of year," she said.

Outside, the April wind wafted through budding apple trees around the Zenner farmstead. Now and then, a gust stirred the topsoil into the air. Birds followed the tractors and lit on the ground to make a meal of insects that the plows had exposed.

"And besides," said Katherine, warming to my nosiness, "I like company and conversation."

Her husband, Al Zenner, was the eldest son of the late John Peter Zenner, who came to the United States several decades ago from Luxembourg, via England, and found farming to his liking. John Peter and his wife, Gertrude, had ten children: six boys and four girls.

"The boys became farmers. . . . All of them."

I sensed that Katherine liked to talk about the family she married into on June 9, 1942. She and Al had three children. The heritage spanned four generations, was rooted in farming, and had been cultivated by elders like Katherine.

"This house was dedicated to our grandchildren and we've had some real nice evenings here," she said. "When we have the Zenner reunions, there's a hundred and two of us."

Katherine's decision to be a farmwife came with some sacrifice. A 1937 graduate of the University of Washington, she held a degree in education and had notched up a couple years of teaching experience before she met Al in Uniontown, Washington.

"I'm an old gym teacher," she said. She also coached girls' basketball. "My Saint Marie's girls' team were the north Idaho champions back then."

We took a walk outside. Al came growling by with a harrow in tow and waved. "He was so happy the day after

Easter 'cause he could get on the tractor. This out here is going to be seeded to peas," Katherine said.

We walked over to the corral and she put a halter on Bell, her Appaloosa mare. Watching her work with the horse, I thought of Diane and her horses.

Katherine had started riding at the age of three and entertained no intentions of quitting. I thought of my wife again. I loved to watch Diane ride and recalled that during our courtship I paid special attention to how her derriere dressed up a saddle.

"I'm still a member of the National Cow Belles," Katherine said, interrupting my reverie.

The wind, still carrying some of winter's sting, slapped us in the face. "The weather over the years has started to get colder in this country," Katherine said matter-of-factly as we shivered our way back to the house. Al was growling around somewhere over the horizon. The apple trees leaned east with the wind. I sensed that Katherine had been working long enough to enjoy a sense of belonging, of knowing that the hands she turned in the kitchen were as important to the farm as the plows that turned the soil.

I shook both of Katherine's hands with both of mine. She nodded and gave me a little bag filled with warm cookies. I ate them all before I got home.

"Guess what," I told Diane in between bites at dinner that night. "I met someone like you, someone you'd like to know, someone you'll probably be like when you get old. Her name is Katherine. She's a farmwife."

— • —

I'm not sure what separates country people from city folks or whether living in one place is better than living in the other. Diane and I chose Hatter Creek's countrified

131

lifestyle and never looked back. Occasionally, though, I've wondered if, by doing so, we limited ourselves to too narrow a perspective.

"Do you think we might be raising our daughters too far from the other end of the spectrum?" I once asked Diane.

She looked at me like I was suddenly a stranger, but I couldn't help it. Sometimes I worried that we might not be giving the kids the kind of opportunities they needed to survive in the real world.

"They know about the world," Diane said.

"Oh sure, remember when we took them to Minneapolis and went downtown? All four of us were gawking up at the skyscrapers like we were the Beverly Hillbillies or something."

"So, what are you saying, that you'd rather raise our kids in a city?" Diane asked, bewildered.

"No, I just hope they understand that they aren't trapped here, that they live here with us because we *choose* to live here. I just worry a little about that."

— • —

Sherry Morgan helped provide some perspective on this issue when she granted me an interview in a location called, of all things, New York Gulch.

"My parents are out in the field," she explained when I arrived.

It was harvest time and nineteen-year-old Sherry had come home from college for the summer to assume her traditional tasks and make some decisions about her future.

"I do all the jobs like cooking and making lunches," she said. "I'll be out in the field some."

Sherry grew up on a wheat farm. During the harvest, she explained, New York Gulch was a "hot and dirty" place that left sweat and dust caked on the entire family, including her dog, Napoleon. As she talked with Napoleon at her side, heat waves and dust devils rose from the fields where combines eased into the fourth day of a two- or three-weeklong harvest season.

Sherry had grown up with a simple job description: farm kid. She lived so far off the beaten path that she was always first on the school bus in the morning and last off at night.

"I was the only kid out here," she said, recalling the fifty miles she rode each way to get to school at Pomeroy, Washington, and the more than two hours she spent every day on the bus.

New York Gulch is the name of a dry streambed that runs from the plateau farm country west of Pomeroy, Washington, down to Central Ferry along the Snake River. Sherry was raised, along with her older brothers, on the Morgan farmstead that their great-grandfather worked. Sherry's dad, Claud, and her mother, Ethel Mae, had worked the place for some two decades. The farm dated back to the turn of the century and was located in a grove of aging shade trees about five miles north of Dodge Junction.

As a child, Sherry recalled, she had no real playmates. "It didn't really bother me to be alone. I liked it. I had my animals. I love cats. . . . I was with my cats all the time."

She remembered playing at home with her Barbie dolls as a little girl and using the CB radio to maintain contact with Mom and Dad out in the fields.

"I always liked to ride in the grain truck when I was little."

Sherry, I realized, was like Heidi and Greta in many ways. She learned to ride a bike on gravel roads, raised chickens, belonged to 4-H, and sometimes wondered what it would be like elsewhere.

"In high school, I always wished I could live in town." But the farm, she said, was a place where she'd learned the value of hard work and how to begin building a life of her own. "I always wanted to work. I'm not afraid of the outside world at all," she said. When she compared her childhood to that of a city kid, Sherry said there was really no comparison.

"I think I have something over them. I think it would be a lot harder to come from a big city to something smaller. Hopefully, I can stay in a rural community. I don't like big cities."

At the time I first interviewed Sherry, Heidi was eight and Greta was just four. I told them both about Sherry and her dog, Napoleon, and all the dust devils in New York Gulch.

"We ride the school bus for almost an hour too," Heidi reminded me.

"Not me," said Greta.

"You're too little," said Heidi.

Both my daughters, I thought, were too little to know there was a much bigger world out there. In a way, I hoped they'd shun the city and thereby verify the decision Diane and I had made to make our home on Hatter Creek.

But Sherry convinced me that my fretting was unnecessary. She eventually moved from the tiny gulch with the big-city name to the town of Cheney, Washington. She finished college, got a job, married Jeff Mowatt, and became the mother of three sons. Some fourteen years after we talked on that hot July day in New York Gulch, Sherry told me she had no romantic notions about life on the farm.

"I can admit that I'm very glad I don't work on a farm anymore," she said. Her parents still owned the spread. But they'd retired and one of her brothers had taken over. Sherry was working as a secretary at Eastern Washington

University in the College of Letters, Arts & Social Sciences. And while she'd never go back to the farm to live, she attributed her successful urban transition to growing up in that hot and dusty gulch.

"Living there, it gave me the ethics of getting up in the morning at the same time and going to work. I was just raised that way. Jeff and I do the same thing today. And even though our boys don't live on the farm, they see us, the way we work, and that's good for them."

— • —

Ultimately, I figured out that it doesn't matter if children grow up in the city or on a farm, as long as their parents give them the love and direction they need, along with the opportunity to make their own choices about what the world offers.

For Diane, the world need not extend too far beyond the fence lines that surrounded our property. And those fence lines have always been a source of contention between us—both literally and figuratively. My job made me venture beyond them. But Diane chose her niche within. And the very maintenance of those fences underscored our differences.

"Sometimes I think all you want from me is to make your dream farm come true," I railed one day when Diane insisted I build a fence line for the horses and use nothing but wooden posts. "Why can't we just buy some steel fence posts?"

Sensing I was in one of those harried moods caused by pending deadlines and the logistics of being a roving reporter, Diane tried to be patient. "I hate the way they look. I love the old, wooden fences."

"Sometimes I get darn tired of trying to make this place

into Funky Farm. What's wrong with Functional Farm? What's wrong with steel fence posts?"

Looking back, the argument was stupid, but it recurred whenever a horse or a deer broke through a fence and I had to pull another wooden post from the treatment barrel filled with oil, dig a hole in the hard ground, and repair the damage. Sometimes the spats went beyond fencing. When we built the barn, we argued for two days about where the windows should go and how wide the doors needed to be. Diane wanted wood boards; I preferred metal siding.

"If there's a hard way to do something, we'll do it. Right?"

"No, I just take a lot of pride in this place," Diane countered. "It's our home. You knew that when you married me. Please don't tell me now that you'd be happier living in the city."

— • —

I wish I more intimately shared the dreams of the lifestyle Diane always longed for. But I must admit that city life probably spoiled me, to the point of not even appreciating the satisfaction of working the ground and getting dirt under my fingernails.

"Did your mother ever plant a garden?" I asked Diane one day while trying to get the rototiller started.

"I don't know. I don't remember her planting one, unless she did when I was really little," said Diane. "I don't know if she was able to, or if she was too sick by then. Daddy always had a garden. He always planted things."

"Is that where you got your obsession with gardening and building and making this place into some sort of statement?"

"It's not an obsession," Diane said, obviously wounded

by my insensitivity. "It's just something I like to do. I love to make things grow. And I want this place to grow with the two of us."

A reasonable viewpoint, I conceded, as I made what I hoped were the final adjustments to the rototiller's temperamental engine. But I still didn't like gardening. Too slow, watching plants grow.

"Besides, you can buy like ten pounds of potatoes for hardly nothing, compared to all the work and sweat you put into growing them."

"But fresh vegetables are so good for us. All I ask you to do is till the garden in the spring," said Diane.

"I don't know if I'll ever understand it," I grumped, finally yanking the rototiller engine to a start.

— • —

I only began to understand the joys of cultivating the soil when I met Earl Bryant, an eighty-one-year-old California transplant with a bean-stalk build.

When I found him, Earl, seemingly with green thumbs on both hands, was leaning on his garden hoe. He peered out from beneath a straw hat with a brim wide enough to cast shade for both of us. I asked what brought him to the far end of the Banana Belt.

"You know," he said, winking at me as I squinted into a warm May sun. "We've never found a banana here."

Among farmers and gardeners alike, the low-lying reach of the Clearwater River drainage in northern Idaho is known as the "Banana Belt." Nearly 2,000 feet lower in elevation from the surrounding plateaus above the steep river breaks, the Banana Belt is known for its warm temperatures, lengthy growing season, and bumper crops of corn, beans, melons, potatoes, zucchini, and just about any other garden delight—except bananas.

"I do believe it's going to be a good garden year," said Earl, gazing toward the sky. Having sown fifty-two gardens during his lifetime, Earl spoke from experience. And now, in the little upriver town of Kooskia at the eastern edge of the Banana Belt, Earl had found paradise.

"I never had such an ideal place in my life."

There was an enthusiasm in Earl's declaration that was contagious. I actually felt like getting down on my hands and knees with him to explore the moist dirt where the worms were thriving and the spinach was already growing.

"I've never been much of a gardener," I confessed. "Just ask my wife. She plants a garden every year and I never set foot in it, except when the rototiller drags me around to get the soil in shape. And she scolds me for not appreciating the wonder of things that grow." I told him that Diane stoops over her work for hours on end, grubbing around in the dirt.

Earl nodded knowingly and explained it this way. "We started growing gardens when I was a boy, so we had something to eat during the Depression. Then I got to where I couldn't get through a year without a garden. It got in my blood." He'd spent forty years painting houses for a living. It was work. His half-century of gardening, on the other hand, was pure play.

"When everything is growing . . . that's the happy part of your life," he said. "You can't keep from just studying it and watching it." Then he leaned even harder on his hoe and looked around at his work to date. "I'm at home out here in the dirt."

Earl planted his garden across the street from his home and adjacent to the Presbyterian church on land the congregation and neighbors invited him to use. "When we moved here, some of these guys wanted to know if I knew anything about gardening."

People, it seemed, were having problems bringing their turnips along and getting their tomatoes to ripen.

"Well, I think their problem was that they left the wife to do all the gardening," Earl suggested. Hmmm . . . hearing that, I reflected that Earl better not utter such a sentiment within earshot of Diane.

Earl's wife, Lereleen, confirmed that she steered clear of the garden until harvest time. "I do all the canning," she said.

Pantry inventory aside, Earl had additional proof of his gardening prowess: a picture of a 105-pound pumpkin he'd grown the year before as well as other shots of corn towering toward the clouds and tomato plants laden with fruit.

"My tomatoes do good. That might sound like bragging," said Earl. "But it's the truth." Phosphorus is the key, he said. It must be added to the ground before the frost to ensure ripe tomatoes. "Some people don't believe in using minerals. They have to use all natural stuff."

Earl also laced his garden with about four inches of cow and sheep droppings. Horse apples also worked well, he claimed, if allowed to mellow at least a year before spreading.

"We have such a wonderful chance this year," he beamed. Right around May tenth Earl planned to put his tomato plants in the garden. The eggplants and peppers would also be set about the same time. Then, the corn and carrots and lettuce would come along and, near the end of July, he'd plant turnips for an early autumn harvest.

"Corn, string beans, pole beans, potatoes, tomatoes, peppers, cabbage, carrots, beats, turnips . . ." The garden would soon burst into a cornucopia of vegetables. Before I left, Earl urged me to return in July.

"You'd see a real garden, then," he said.

I never did return. Six years after we talked, and about the time another growing season was ready to begin, Earl suffered a stroke. He lingered for three months. Then, early in July when the corn was supposed to be knee-high, Earl died of pneumonia.

His obituary read: "He enjoyed fishing, but his main hobby was gardening and sharing his produce with friends and neighbors." Earl was buried in the Pine Grove Cemetery. His garden, adjacent to the Presbyterian church, reverted back to grass and small trees.

Here was a man who, with a cultivator and other gardening implements, had made the world more beautiful. When he died, Idaho lost a little of its beauty.

Last summer, while making a rare stop at the farmers' market in Moscow, I bought a handmade sign for Diane's garden, just to show her I finally accepted her zest for growing things, even if I didn't understand it. The sign reads: *Stop and Smell the Flowers.*

I've yet to participate in the planting of Diane's garden. The pace doesn't and probably never will suit me. I guess I prefer more immediate gratification, the kind that comes with opening a can of corn or ordering a baked potato with my steak dinner. But thanks to Earl, I'm trying to heed the writing on that sign I bought for my wife's garden.

— • —

I climbed aboard Allis again recently. She was in a deep coma, having spent yet another winter parked in the pasture. A front tire was flat. The battery was dead. I cranked the engine over by hand.

"Come on, damn it, start."

Nothing.

I peered into the gasoline tank.

Empty.

The soup can atop the exhaust pipe rattled around in the wind.

"Well, Allis," I said out loud. "I hope you're just sleeping."

Then I poked around at the engine, all greasy and cold. As much as I didn't relish going through the routine again, I decided to set a date once again to resurrect the little orange tractor. With the arrival of spring, there'd be work waiting for her.

And I knew, if nothing else, that the sound of the engine would bring a smile to Diane's face.

CHAPTER SIX

Work

No matter how I punched the calculator's little keys, the bottom line remained red.

"I really don't know how we're going to make it," I moaned. "We just keep living beyond our means."

Diane said nothing. Money was not her favorite subject. Mine either. The only subject I hated worse was lack of money. And staring me in the face was the bottom line of our financial situation. The way I saw it, we had three options: I find a way to make more money, we cut our costs, or Diane goes to work.

"David, we've talked about this before. We agreed that my place is here. Greta just started school and Heidi's only in the fifth grade . . . and I've got all the animals to tend. Maybe you could get a raise."

"The *Trib* is struggling too. I can't go in there and ask for a raise. Everybody in the newsroom would like a raise. I'm just thankful I've got a job."

"Well, so am I. And you know, it's not like I don't work around here."

I thumped my head down on the table, rubbed the back

of my neck with one hand, and tapped my pen with the other.

"I know, I know. We've been over this ground before. I'm not saying you don't work hard here, but the bottom line is—"

"I hate these bottom-line conversations."

So did I. We covered the same ground over and over again, and usually ended up in the same place: I'd suggest Diane get a job as a secretary, and she'd remind me she couldn't type, and even if she could, she despised the claustrophobic monotony of office work. (She often said working in a butcher shop appealed to her more.) I'd say we needed more money, and she'd say her job was to raise the girls.

The thing is, both of us were right. I knew Diane wasn't afraid of work. She worked all the time making a home for us. Hour for hour, she spent more time on the job than I did. But I was angry.

"Well fine." I pouted. "I guess we'll just let the place go under. Funky Farm will become Rundown Ranch and then, when the time comes, you can pound the 'For Sale' sign on a tree."

Around and around went the argument. And, always, Diane would stand her ground: Before anything else, she was a mom. I guess I had problems understanding that—how she could define herself as a career mom.

While making a living as a roving reporter, I've driven the equivalent of twenty times around the world. I've met butchers and bakers, even a candlestick maker, truck drivers, teachers, lawyers, laborers, doctors, nurses, repairmen, waitresses, cosmetologists, used-car salesmen, carpenters, and a guy who made a living by dressing up as a nerd to deliver singing telegrams.

Our jobs, especially if we work them by choice, reveal

much of who and maybe even what we are. People know me as David Johnson, "that reporter." My neighbor is Bob Carpenter, the rancher. My good friend is John Prideaux, the retired parole officer. Our friend down the road is Barb Coyner, the freelance writer.

But who, sometimes I asked, was Diane? Why had she failed to prepare herself for work outside the home? With what, other than motherhood, holding down the farm, and being my wife, did she identify?

I hated myself for asking these questions of the woman I loved. But I wasn't the only one: Diane's high school art teacher loved her dearly but shared some of my frustration.

"She's just so talented," Juanita always said when we talked about Diane's artistic leanings. "I wish she'd draw and paint more."

I encouraged Diane to draw again, maybe even for money.

"I don't have the passion to do that right now," Diane answered. "To do that, I'd just have to drop everything else. I can't just stop, become an artist, and make money. There's too much unfinished business around me. I'm distracted by all that goes into building the house and the inconveniences."

Passion is indeed a pithy word, the most succinct summation of what Mary Kirkwood put into her works—and what I hoped Diane could find within herself someday. A retired professor of art at the University of Idaho, Mary was best known as a painter of portraits. The entire human body in all its naked wonder, said Mary, had always caught her eye. Because she'd deliberated for so long on what she called the "human figure," Mary was able to paint beyond clothes and nakedness to the innermost qualities of human nature.

"It's the most beautiful art in the world. . . . I'm afraid

there are a great number of people who think art is any-thing," Mary said, glancing up at one of her works on the wall. "Maybe something ugly can be art, but not because it's simply ugly." After devoting her entire life to the study of the great masters and the development of her own tal-ents, Mary was convinced that art must be an expression, not just a pretty picture.

"A painting must communicate," she said. "It takes a great deal of understanding, and yet, it may be impossible to say this is art and this isn't art. I consider myself more a teacher than an artist. My teaching came first. I don't have any pretensions about my ability. I feel I've become a mod-est artist.

"I loved teaching," said Mary, "but painting was my pas-sion."

Mary died at the age of ninety and her paintings, as it is with so many artists, suddenly became more valuable. I've always wanted to buy one of her works, if for no other rea-son than to remind me that paintings might be valuable, but artists—even those who've yet to tap the recesses of their talent—are quite priceless.

"There will be a time," Diane assured me, "but I can't be creative amid chaos. I need to get this part of my life com-pleted. Then I'll take the time. Do you understand that?"

Who was I to try to exploit what Diane had yet to un-lock? If she were to become an artisan, it would be at her own initiative. I just hoped she'd take the time while she still could.

— • —

Sometimes, while roving the region, I park at the crest of the Lewiston Hill to think about my work. Most tourists veer into the scenic overlook, grab their cameras, and start shooting. But I've learned to gaze beyond the view and notice the pulse of commerce.

The mighty Snake and Clearwater Rivers frame the scene below. The cities of Lewiston, Idaho, and Clarkston, Washington, sprawl around the confluence of the two waterways. Just upstream from the confluence, the Tribune Building is but a speck in the landscape. Beyond that, the Potlatch Corporation sawmill and paper plant, with all its buildings, smokestacks, and thousands of employees, pumps the economic lifeblood of the valley.

Over the years, I've interviewed dozens of people employed by Potlatch. But no one has stuck with me quite like Nancy Elsbury of Peck, Idaho.

Nancy was in charge of quality control at Potlatch.

In the toilet paper division.

I had visions of a corporate outhouse located in the bowels of the Potlatch plant—a privy stationed next to an assembly line flanked by baskets marked "Pass" and "Fail." For the life of me, I couldn't comprehend how someone could say with a straight face that she was a toilet paper tester.

"Actually, I take more jokes because I'm from Peck than I do for making toilet paper," Nancy said. "I mean, what do you call a person from Peck?"

I had a few ideas.

"A Peckite," Nancy said before scolding me for having my mind in the gutter.

Before the interview she had taken the precaution of calling some higher-ups for the okay. In no time they agreed, much to my surprise. I'd expected a bigger fight, considering the dignified image most companies like to project. But I soon realized that Nancy Elsbury of Peck occupied a unique spot in the Potlatch pecking order. After all, her work had universal application.

———

"A lot of people fondly tell me how they used to use the Sears catalog," Nancy deadpanned. "But I don't know anyone today who doesn't use toilet paper."

I don't know anyone who'd *admit* they didn't use toilet paper, I thought.

And then, before taking me on a tour of Potlatch's multimillion-dollar toilet paper complex, Nancy summed up what experience had taught her about the human race.

"I've found that the world is divided into two kinds of people," she declared. "Crumplers and folders."

I was about halfway through writing down the quote when I began to smile and looked up to see Nancy, all dressed in tweed and looking as corporate as the next guy, smiling back.

"My observation," she explained, "well, I shouldn't say my observation . . . but from my random conversations, I understand people either fold or crumple a handful that feels right."

She didn't even blush about her research findings. I tried my best to register all this with a solemn nod. But then she came back with yet another inside joke about Potlatch's being accused of making John Wayne toilet paper: "Rough, tough, and won't take crap off anybody." The conversation, it seemed, was destined to be one of double entendres.

Dilating on the technical aspects of her job, Nancy pointed out that cedar trees make the softest bathroom tissue.

I squirmed.

Chipped, soaked, and aged just right, cedar-tree fiber apparently works just dandy. Nancy, a college chemistry graduate, explained that the molecular structure of cedar lends itself to the qualities most sought in bathroom tissue, like softness.

When you think about it, turning any tree into something as personal and as universally used as toilet paper is a small miracle—one rarely appreciated by the everyday consumer who folds or crumples and flushes without a second thought.

All fun aside, Nancy was someone who'd moved up to a management-level job not just because she could tell good toilet paper jokes, but because she was talented and developed a repertoire of skills well beyond taking informal surveys on crumplers and folders. Upon graduation in 1978 from Utah State University at Logan, she took a chemist's job with Westinghouse-Hanford Company near Richland, Washington. She and others on a scientific team worked to develop a method for disposing of nuclear-contaminated equipment. Then she married her husband, John, whom she'd met in college.

Nancy admitted to some misgivings about her career track. "When I got this job making toilet paper, I felt like I'd abandoned my social responsibility. But when you think about it, where would we be without toilet paper?"

Thoughts of those Sears catalogs and corncobs raced through my head.

"It's a lot easier to get along without nuclear power and it's a lot easier to dispose of toilet paper," she said.

So we took the tour, a quick run-through of the Potlatch tissue paper plant, dodging forklifts, shouting questions and answers above the roar of machinery, ogling the enormity of the entire operation. The "Number Two" paper machine was turning out huge cylinders of bathroom tissue called "parent rolls" at a rate of fifty-seven miles' worth an hour. I wondered for a moment if Paul Bunyan was a crumpler or a folder.

Then we went through a door and entered a virtually soundproof control center where machine tender Jim Long and several other men were monitoring the paper machine's output on a computer. The terminal was stationed amid a futuristic-looking control panel with knobs, switches, and blinking lights.

"This is all day-one equipment," Nancy said, pointing out that the paper machine was brought on line in 1980. One of the men told me that Nancy had earned their respect not just because she helped perfect and understood the paper machine better than most, but because she'd paid her dues.

"She's the greatest target for a water hose that ever walked the plant," he said.

As one of the parent rolls grew to nearly 3,500 pounds, Nancy and the others tried to put it all in perspective. One of the rolls could blanket U.S. Highway 12 from Lewiston to one-half mile short of Orofino. That's about forty-one miles and enough toilet paper to supply three families for three generations.

Finally, Nancy took me to the place I'd really been waiting to see: the quality-control lab. But instead of a dark and dank outhouse with toilet paper rolls sealed in used coffee cans, it was a brightly lit room with rolls of toilet paper on shelves. She took down a roll to do some tests as I watched.

First, Nancy placed a sheet in a little $18,000 pulling machine to test the perforation strength. The roll passed.

There was a simpler test for softness.

"Want to feel?" she asked, offering me a touch of tissue.

Then she demonstrated a third test for checking whether two-ply toilet paper will separate into single ply, which could result in rejection.

"This is not a real scientific test," she said, unrolling six sheets' worth and waving them back and forth eight times. Only one sheet separated. The roll passed.

At the close of the interview, I couldn't resist asking, well, the obvious question. Nancy looked me straight in the eye. "I'm a crumpler."

Like I said, I've met the loggers, administrators, and janitors at Potlatch. But Nancy, Queen of Quality Control, was one of a kind.

— • —

Over the years, I've watched the industrial revolution of loggers, trees, and private companies wind to a close, replaced by the digital age of dot-coms, the Internet, and megaconglomerates. My first encounter with job instability came in the mid-1980s, when the *Lewiston Morning Tribune*'s ownership underwent drastic change that unsettled the newsroom and homes like ours. Two branches of the Alford family decided to sell. Publisher A. L. Butch Alford, Jr., wanted to keep the newspaper but didn't have the financial wherewithal. So the other family members sold their stock to the Kerns-Tribune Corporation of Salt Lake City, owner of the *Salt Lake Tribune*.

As long as Butch remained publisher, I figured I'd have a job. But if the Salt Lake bean counters decided to cut costs, they'd look pretty hard at the older reporters.

"Why would anyone want to get rid of a good reporter?" Diane asked.

The newsroom, I tried to explain, was not immune to the economic and technological changes that were sweeping the country.

"The industrial revolution, believe it or not, is ancient history. It's given way to the computer era that's exploding all around us. You can see the fallout in the timber and farming industries. People are being sucked into an economic maelstrom. It's Darwinian. It's survival of the fittest. Loggers are losing their jobs. Farmers are losing their farms. People are moving away. The spin-off is shrinking *Tribune* circulation numbers. The paper is hurting. . . . It's vulnerable."

"But the *Tribune* is a good newspaper. Why would anyone want to buy it and wreck it?" asked Diane, frustrated with the growing reality that along with the *Tribune's* future would go our livelihood.

I tried to reassure her. But I couldn't kick thoughts about the kids and responsibility, the mortgage, the car payment—and I couldn't bear to think about leaving the *Tribune* with a pink slip rather than a retirement party. Like most writers, my thoughts of the future run the gamut from "I have to buy gas tomorrow" to elaborate, multi-tiered scenarios of success and failures. One of my favorite fantasies is of my retirement.

When I call it quits, I ask for only two things. First, I'd like to see a very small story on the front page announcing to our readers that I've had it. I'm done. Second, I'd like the entire newsroom to attend a brief ceremony. The gathering would take place sometime after midnight on the day of my retirement. Everybody would meet in the pressroom as tomorrow's newspaper, the one with my retirement story, was rolling off the press.

In the midst of the noise and excitement, we'd all stand with champagne bottles and glasses in hand. And at the pinnacle of the commotion, when the entire Tribune Building was shaking with the roar of free speech, Publisher Butch Alford would raise a bottle high into the air and shout, "All right. In honor of a damn good reporter named David Johnson, stop the presses!"

With that, the big Goss Urbanite would grind and groan to a halt until silence filled the air. Everybody would shake my hand, pat me on the back and—that would be it. The press would restart, my former co-workers would go back to their jobs, and I'd go home.

———

In my fantasy as I exited the door someone would say, "Way to go, DJ."

Shirley Cook of Lenore, Idaho, sparked this retirement idea. For Shirley, retirement wasn't a matter of nest eggs in the bank or travel plans. It was about retrieving her old mop bucket as a memento and garnering kind comments from lots of people, "including the supervisors and big shots."

For more than a quarter of a century, Shirley had been a fixture at a bullet manufacturing plant called Blount Inc. The company was the third largest employer in Lewiston, Idaho, and Shirley had been in charge of the lunchroom. She confessed to being like a doting mom to hundreds of employees.

"I like people," she explained. "I sat in the same spot for twenty-five years. I moved once . . . and they had a frantic fit."

When Shirley finally retired, she got a gold watch. More important, she got to keep her old mop bucket.

"I scrubbed clear around the world," she said, sighing. Somebody painted the bucket and Shirley made it into a magazine rack.

"I worked really hard there. Not because they demanded it. But I thought it would look good on my record if I wanted to clean somewhere else. And I'm just that way. I like to keep busy."

Retirement, said Shirley, shouldn't be sought or shunned. It should just happen—a natural winding down of our workaday lives into something worth remembering. In Shirley's case, retirement came a couple of years early because her husband of forty-five years, Larry, had taken ill. Her premature parting, Shirley said, gave Blount a good excuse to throw a great big company party. Being appreciated that much, said Shirley, made leaving even more difficult.

The Blount lunchroom wasn't just a place to eat. It was 4,200 square feet of floor space where hundreds of people at a time tried to make the most of their precious minutes away from the job.

"We had a dollar machine, but I was faster making change," said Shirley. She did everything from keeping the coffeepots perking to baking hundreds of TV dinners brought by people from home for lunch.

"I have a lot of scars to prove it," said Shirley, exposing the burn marks on her forearms from getting too close to the oven. "It was the only place in the world where people got monogrammed pot pies," said Shirley, explaining how she used an ice pick to carve people's names on the pies before baking to make sure everyone got the dinner they brought.

"Some days, when someone was down or not feeling good, I'd put a message on their pot pies to cheer them up. That's the kind of thing I miss doing now. They were just part of the family to me."

When it came time for the retirement party, Shirley was overwhelmed. "I couldn't believe how many people came." In addition to the mop bucket and gold watch, she received a lot of other gifts and the kind of send-off that still brought tears to her eyes.

"They keep saying, 'Shirley, when are you coming back to visit?' And I say, 'Oh, in the spring. Give me a chance to be away awhile.'"

Shirley stayed away for some six years, visiting her place of employment just a couple of times, before we talked again. Her husband had died and she now lived alone doing "lots and lots of yard work." There was a hint of contentment in her voice when I asked about the old job and she told me they had to install a lot more coffeemakers and microwaves after she retired. "I'd have to do about one-eighth the work now. I sure worked myself to death there. But it was just part of my job."

Most of us, when and if we find our niche in the work world, will indeed work ourselves almost to death. If we're lucky, that commitment will yield not just internal, but external rewards. Then again, economic forces can sometimes create a send-off ruder than the one Shirley experienced.

By the time I started my column in 1984, the once-booming forest industry was fighting for survival. Stories about laid-off loggers kept leaping like obituaries from the phone book. I wrote not just about individual lumberjacks, but also about gyppo logging outfits and mills that had fallen on hard times. Eventually, the white pages led me to a woman who stood with grief etched across her face and reminisced about the death of an entire town. Not only had her dreams of a secure retirement faded, but her very *home* was fading before her eyes.

"It looks so terribly woebegone," sighed Zella Cantrell as she gazed around the defunct Headquarters General Store, walked behind the remnant snack counter, and nudged aside some debris with her foot.

Amid the clutter of what used to be the town hub, precious memories seemed to spar with the need to move ahead. "I'm optimistic," said Zella. "I look forward. I don't get that nostalgic. Oh, when they burn it down, like I say, I'll probably have a few pangs."

Headquarters, Idaho, was a company town. It thrived as a logging community and served as gatekeeper to Idaho's expansive North Fork timber region. Zella and her husband, Gary, operated the town's only store for some eighteen years.

"In the good old days, I'd put forty to sixty cases of pop and beer in the cooler every night," Zella said. That's how brisk business was when the timber industry boomed into the late 1970s.

By the mid-1980s, Headquarters was still home for scores of families who worked for Potlatch Corporation. The biggest forest-industry employer in north central Idaho, Potlatch owned the town, including all the houses. Residents were from workaday families with ties to the community dating back to pre-Depression days, when the railroad blasted and bridged its way through the wilderness to finally link the area to the outside world.

At one time, more than a thousand men were said to have worked out of Headquarters in logging camps radiating up into the mountains like spokes on a wagon wheel. Draft horses hauled payloads of logs back down for transfer onto rail cars. Some of the trees that fell were so big that the logs had to be taken out of the mountains one at a time.

Remoteness forced Headquarters into complete self-reliance. In the earlier days there was a school, a community center, a blacksmith shop, and even an electric plant that worked until the late 1940s, when power lines finally arrived.

And of course, the general store. Zella ushered me through its remains on a late June day in 1988, some two years after Potlatch Corporation had announced the indefinite curtailment of logging in the region. Even though logging would eventually resume, the layoff signaled the beginning of the end for the company town that hundreds called home.

"The whole area up here is kind of passing history," Zella said. The Cantrells arrived in Headquarters in 1969 with their four year old daughter, Caren. The town jumped with prosperity.

"The way they were logging in 1969 and the early 1970s,

it was almost not unlike the gold rush," she said. Indeed, gold fever back in the mid-1800s sent miners by the thousands into the Clearwater and Salmon River regions of what was then Washington Territory. When the Northern Pacific Railway Company finally punched a spur to Pierce and on through to Headquarters, trees by the millions, not gold by the ounce, proved more valuable.

"I don't know anyone in the area who had financial troubles," Zella said of how the timber industry sustained the residents of both Headquarters and neighboring Pierce into the seventies. "It was sort of the boom years."

I snapped some pictures of Zella as she poked through the remains of her store, figuring this was her last chance before the match was struck. A couple of years earlier, when logging was still humming, I met a logger named David McIntosh at the store. He and members of his three-man crew had agreed to escort me into the forest the next morning against company policy to do a story about the last tree falling before the big layoff.

I don't recall seeing Zella at the store. But she remembered my story and lamented that Headquarters was by that time fast becoming a shell of what it used to be. That's why she and her husband decided to close the store. They could see the company town spinning toward demise as lumber markets continued to slump and people moved away.

Zella was forty-four years old. Gary was forty-five. The store seemed ageless. A wood-framed structure, it had been stocked with all the items necessary to live in logging country—everything from chainsaw oil, ax handles, and hard hats to groceries, beer, and chewing tobacco.

People in Headquarters rented their houses from the company, but invested their lives in one another. The workday usually began between 3:30 and 4 A.M. as loggers, nursing cups of coffee and guiding pickup trucks into the darkness, headed for the woods. During the daylight hours, the town bustled with timber-industry business. By nine at night all was quiet, as everyone, even the children, respected the working man's need for rest.

"The people up here are pretty much a little group of their own," Zella said. As a storeowner, she catered to a genuine sense of community and took pride in her citizenry.

"There was a whole generation of kids I watched grow up. If their kids were sick and Mom wasn't home, they called the store." Even small-town gossip didn't detract from overall friendliness. "Along with the nosiness comes the caring," Zella said. But all of it, including her store, was becoming part of a bygone era.

"It looks so forlorn with all the stuff gutted out," grieved Zella, standing as if frozen in thought, or perhaps in time. The electric clock over the snack counter had stopped at 12:25—A.M. or P.M., it didn't seem to matter. What remained of the lunch menu on the wall read: *Hamburger dlx $2.25*.

The Cantrells had lived above the store in a modest apartment with a window that overlooked the company parking lot, the town baseball field, and the forests beyond. Like everyone else who worked directly or indirectly in the timber industry, Zella had her own ideas about why hard times came and clung to the region.

"It just isn't economically feasible to have a company town." She shrugged. "It's hard to be objective when you've lived here. I would like it to remain the last company town. I always enjoyed the little place."

Then Zella turned and walked out the store's back door, never to return again.

Potlatch Corporation eventually tore down and burned the entire town of Headquarters—first the company bunkhouses, then the cook shack, Zella's store, and finally the homes. One by one, families had to move away. Zella and Gary moved down the road to Cardiff Spur, where they bought and still operate the Hunt Oil Company bulk plant.

— • —

After Zella's story ran, Diane and I both admitted that we had it pretty good, retirement fantasy or not. Getting behind on the bills was one thing. Losing a business, home, and community was another. What we admired most about Zella was her adaptability in devising another way to make ends meet. That's what we needed to do: stop fretting about what had become of our financial situation and do something about it.

"I'll admit it," I told Diane. "I don't bring home enough money. That's the only reason I'm bugging you about getting a job. Believe me, it is."

Every now and then, Diane seemed to be listening to my pleas, to the point where I worried halfheartedly that she might just leave the home front behind. Like the day she picked up the *Tribune*, read my column, and declared, "Now here's a woman who's doing something I can relate to."

The story was about Elma Qualey, who lived in Grangeville, Idaho.

"The next time you climb aboard your favorite Ray Holes saddle," I'd written, "think of seventy-two-year-old Elma. More likely than not, your rump will be cradled in her handiwork."

Diane put down the paper and gazed out the window. "I could see myself working in a place like Ray Holes."

The Ray Holes Saddle Company had been located for decades in downtown Grangeville. As the story goes, Ray

Holes built his first saddle around 1933, but then spent another three years traveling the West to really learn the art from veteran saddle makers. He returned to Grangeville in 1936 and opened a shop.

Among people like my wife who know horses and tack, a Ray Holes saddle is synonymous with quality.

"I rawhide the saddle trees," Elma said. For almost three decades, she made a living by stretching, pulling, fitting, and sewing rawhide over, under, and around the wooden tree that formed the foundation of a saddle. Her work required strong hands and a commitment to the Frank Lloyd Wright dictum: "Form follows function."

Try as I did, I couldn't imagine Diane, with all her artistic leanings, laboring around in a saddle shop at what amounted to an assembly-line job. Then again, I couldn't deny Elma's enthusiasm for her work. A good saddle, she explained, fits both the rider and the horse as if fusing the two. And a good saddle, she said, should outlive the horse, rider, and maker.

While Elma searched for the exact number of saddles she'd stretched, I admired the saddle she'd propped in the living room of her home like a fine piece of furniture. It belonged to her late husband, Tom Qualey, who also worked for the Ray Holes Saddle Company. In fact, Elma and Tom were teamed up for some two decades at the saddle shop. He fashioned the wooden trees and Elma applied the rawhide covering.

In a way, I thought, Elma was like a good newspaper editor or a stay-at-home mom: Her work was seldom noticed unless something went wrong. The tree of the saddle, she explained, was virtually swallowed up by the layers of leather that went into the finished product.

"One thousand, six hundred and forty-nine," said Elma,

returning from the kitchen. "And I know who just about every one went to."

If we pried a bit on the skirt, she explained, I might get a glimpse of the rawhide underlining and the hefty stitch work that formed the saddle's foundation.

"You can see just a little of it there," grunted Elma as I helped her spread the leather layers on Tom's saddle to reveal some of the rawhide. "See the stitches." Her eyes and voice celebrated the moment, as if exposing the stitches was akin to baring her soul and finding everything in good condition. She seemed genuinely pleased to be just one of several saddle makers who practiced their art.

"Ray Holes himself done that," she said, letting go of the skirts and running her hands over the horn of the saddle and down across all the ornate leatherwork. Elma was hoping to sell the saddle and had put a $900 price tag on it. Anyone willing to cough up the cash, she said, was getting a good deal.

"It's like new."

As for Elma, she conceded being less than new. "The old gray mare"—she cackled, slapping Tom's saddle—"she ain't what she used to be."

Two weeks after our interview, Elma sold Tom's saddle. Then she retired, her hands no longer containing the strength needed to pull and stretch the rawhide into shape. As predicted, the saddle outlived its maker. Elma died of cancer in July of 1997.

When people talk of writers, poets, or artists, they often refer to a body of work. It would be gratifying for someone to pore over my decades of newspaper clippings and in some way applaud them as a body of work. But the work I do is right there for everyone to see and either appreciate or dismiss. In Elma's case, her work was buried under layers of leather. Still, she didn't need anyone to recognize her achievements. She possessed a sense of pride that needed no outside approval.

No wonder Diane liked her story, and maybe even envied her job.

— • —

Just for the heck of it, I looked up the definition of work the other day. The dictionary defined it as "effort to do or make something: labor, toil."

I liked that.

Then I looked up the word *career*. The dictionary called it "one's progress through life."

I liked that even better.

By definition, Diane had embarked on a career long before we met. She knew about labor and toil. She was determined to make progress through life. The only difference was that she, like all "housewives," didn't get a paycheck.

Babs Motley, another woman whose life my column delved into, related to such inequity. Curled up in the corner of the couch where she often sat, Babs rolled her eyes and admitted to being a bit embarrassed about what she'd told me on the telephone a couple days earlier.

"Just a housewife," she repeated, embarrassed at her self-description. "After I hung up, I thought, 'just a housewife,' what a dumb thing to say."

At the time I called, about one hundred journalists had monitored our conversation. I'd been asked to give a talk about my column at the annual Poynter Institute's National Writer's Workshop in Portland. As part of my presentation, someone from the audience selected a number from the telephone book and we dialed from a speaker phone. When Babs answered, she didn't realize she had an audience.

"I was surprised when you finally told me," Babs admitted, blushing.

She was even more surprised to learn that several of the women were beside themselves when she said a housewife didn't have anything interesting to say. They could hardly keep their mouths shut. And when I finally talked her into an interview, they cheered.

Babs squirmed a little tighter into the corner of the couch and quoted Oprah Winfrey. "She says housewives are the mainstay of America."

At fifty-one years old, Babs was a mainstay and more. Not only had she been a homemaker for her husband and two daughters; some eighteen years before my visit, she'd given birth to a brainchild that had matured into a healthy family business.

"I'd thought about it quite a while," she said. "My husband was a workaholic and I thought if he's going to work that much, he might as well work for himself and his family." So Babs and husband Jerry Motley took a ride one evening. He drove, she navigated. They came to vacant ground at the edge of Pullman, Washington, a plotted but undeveloped subdivision called Sunrise Terrace. It was for sale.

"I was working as a bookkeeper and Jerry was working construction. We were both putting in fourteen hours a day." When she looked out over the land, Babs saw the potential to change her family's lifestyle for the better. A few days later, Jerry and his brother, Bill, bought the land. Motley & Motley, a construction business, had been launched.

"There was a lot of sacrifice," said Babs, who credited her husband and brother-in-law with building the business and giving her a chance to become what she'd always wanted to be: "just a housewife."

The title, said Babs, doesn't do justice to the importance—not to mention the constant demands—of the day-to-day job. "A family business," she said, "is still recognized as a bit of Old America." But behind such a business there must be a strong family. And at the center of the family, maintained Babs, must be a person dedicated to making the house a home.

I thought of Diane as I jotted down Babs's words.

— • —

Working-world women have long surrounded me. My editor of more than a decade is a woman. Most of the news reporters at the *Tribune* are women. In fact, women have humbled me with their talents for so long that I sometimes forget the struggle they've waged in the workplace.

But their success has also left men like Ray Bell and me struggling with our own identity.

Well, maybe not Ray so much as me.

"I'm a displaced peanut farmer," Ray told me when I stopped by one day. He lived with his wife, Nancy, not in the country, but in a spacious contemporary home in the heart of Pullman, Washington's university community. Ray had no degree, was working as a homebuilder, and quipped that his title was "good spousal unit."

Nancy, on the other hand, had earned the rambling title of "Washington State University Chair, Department of Finance, Insurance and Real Estate, and Distinguished Professor of Risk Management Insurance." In other words, Nancy was in active pursuit of her career and Ray gladly followed. In a way, I envied him. Nancy seemed to have relieved her husband of all that financial fretting men are supposed to do.

"I feel very fortunate to be a professional woman," said Nancy, who was forty-seven.

I suggested that some men (maybe even myself) might balk at making less money than their wives.

Ray shrugged as if to signal that I'd yet to learn some things about contemporary trends. Nancy, for her part, blushed like a schoolgirl at the idea of Ray being a "nineties" kind of guy.

"He's very macho, traditional in a lot of respects," she said. "I'm attracted to that. And I just want to be with him. Ray has never lacked self-confidence."

The two met in Florida, where Nancy was a professor at Florida State University. Ray was managing a road-striping company, a position he'd secured after financial difficulties drove him and a lot of others out of peanut farming.

"Farming is in the blood," confided Ray. "But it's just not economically feasible."

"I had two friends try to hook me up with him," said Nancy, "and I thought he was too good looking to be nice or to be interested in me."

She was wrong. Ray was indeed interested and the two dated, got engaged, and were married. Their move to Pullman came after WSU advertised an opening in the College of Business. Nancy applied, got the job, and she and Ray, along with their son, Robbie, made the move.

"Someone has to do it," Ray said, acknowledging that contemporary marriages often require that couples sit down and decide who takes the lead. In that respect, I identified more with Nancy than Ray. She'd assumed the lead. She was the breadwinner. She paid the lion's share of the bills. But Nancy had the sensitivity not to question Ray's worth. His lack of academic credentials, for example, never figured into the equation.

"There's certainly not an intelligence difference," she said.

Nor was there any such difference between Diane and

me. But unlike Nancy, I'd questioned my spouse's contribution, and therefore her identity.

— • —

"It's not that I think you're incapable," I tried to explain to Diane. "You work all the time. You make me tired just watching you around here. It's just that—"

"That I don't make money?"

"Well, yes. I mean, you know what I bring home. It doesn't cut it. We can't make ends meet—we . . ."

And then it hit me. If anyone had failed in our traditional relationship, it wasn't Diane. She agreed to stay home. I bought into being the provider. She'd always held up her end of the agreement. And now, after admitting I couldn't do my part, I was asking her—no, *expecting* her—to move beyond the domestic front and become a working-world woman. I thought back on all those heated conversations.

"I'm not going to talk about this anymore," said Diane. "I get too upset. It's not worth it. I don't want to fight about money."

I didn't either. But lack of money was at the root of all our arguments. And the quarrels were getting more frequent, not to mention more hurtful.

"What would you do differently, if you had a chance?" I asked rhetorically one evening.

"Nothing," said Diane without hesitation. "I can be very happy with simple things. I don't need a career to be happy. I don't need a job to feel fulfilled."

"Would you want Heidi and Greta to follow in your footsteps, to do what you've done with your life?"

Diane looked at me, her eyes wounded, then darting

with anger. "What do you mean?" she said, quickly turning her attention back to a pile of laundry she was folding.

"We've always told the girls that college is the key, that they have to get an education to be a success," I said, taking a pair of my underwear from the basket to fold.

"If the girls want to go to school," said Diane, "I'm all for it."

"Want. What do you mean, want? They can't just want to go to school. How can anybody in this day and age have the luxury of wanting to get an education? They must go to school or—"

"Or what?" said Diane, turning from the pile of laundry to confront the attack. "Or what? End up like their mother—uneducated, can't even type, can't cope in the real world, just another housewife? Is that what you mean?"

I didn't answer. Because when I looked at my wife standing there, with her work all around her, defending herself at day's end from the man who was supposed to be her partner, I had no answer. Nothing, anyhow, that would make the bills go away or Diane feel better.

— • —

And then I met Sandy Winters, who'd already fought her way into the working world and was now trying to make a calculated retreat. The return home, she said, had become a battle in its own right.

"Society doesn't put enough value on parenting and staying at home," she said.

Sandy described herself as a contemporary woman who'd initially shunned the domestic front. She'd earned a master's degree in business administration and a bachelor's degree in elementary education.

"There were a couple of years," she recalled, "when I was really on the career track."

Her husband, Kel, was also pursuing a doctoral degree. Then, at the age of thirty, Sandy and Kel had a son. And with the arrival of Chad, Sandy found herself tugged by a mother's natural instinct to be with her child. By the time I talked with her, Chad was five and Sandy had given birth to another son, five-month-old Patrick.

"There are battle lines drawn sometimes between women who work and those who don't," she said. "Economics has forced many people to work just to make ends meet. And I hate to come down on women who do work full time.

"I eventually plan to go back to work someday. But now I have a new baby. I feel comfortable with the choices we've made. I don't know, I may go back to school someday. I may start my own business."

— • —

I'd never envisioned Diane as a businessperson. Business success struck me as the result of people turning something they loved into a moneymaking proposition. And there didn't appear to be any labor unions for homemakers.

So, in my continuing quest to figure how Diane might become the provider of additional income, I thought back to when Heidi and Greta were young and Diane would tell them stories about her first dog. I'd listen from the periphery of these tales and marvel at how the girls hung on every word.

"I named him Terp after the nursery rhyme about a little dog Terp that 'barked so loud that I could not slumber or sleep,'" Diane would say.

The memory lit a lightbulb over my head.

"We've got to do something to get out from under these

bills," I said to Diane one day while getting ready to leave for work. "What do you think—is it time to open Hatter Creek Kennels?"

I'd floated the concept of a small dog-boarding kennel before. But by the tone of my voice, Diane could tell I was serious this time.

"I don't know," she said. "We've never even boarded our own dogs before. Who'd come so far out? How would we get it started?"

"We just get the word out," I said, giving her a quick kiss while going out the door. "People are nuts about their dogs and they'll pay for good care."

Diane followed me out to the car.

"I'm telling you," I said while starting the engine, "you'd be great at this. You're great with dogs. A business like this might get us out of debt. Wouldn't that make you feel good? It would make me feel great!"

"I'll think about it," Diane said as I began to drive away.

"You'd love it. You could be top dog. You could be Dog Woman!"

"Oh, thanks."

"It's a term of endearment, believe me."

And with that, I sped happily down the driveway toward another interview, only to glance in the rearview mirror and see Diane standing there motionless, like she was finally resigned to financial necessity and her life was about to change.

— • —

I got into the newspaper business because I needed a job more than a profession. Once hired, I stopped on the first rung of the so-called career ladder and never sought better-paying editorial or management positions. Like Diane, I was content with "simpler" things. But while roving for

more than two decades in the company Subaru, I sometimes wondered if it was time to stop or at least change direction. It is indeed good to be employed at a job one
enjoys. But during those wearisome stretches, I wondered if
I should have followed another career path.

"I think you're a good reporter," Diane would say, trying
to buck me up.

"What would I be if I *weren't* a reporter, though? Maybe
a teacher . . . or sometimes I think, Why the heck did I get
the degree in wildlife management and then not use it?"

As it happened, my latent curiosity about what it would
be like to work as a wildlife biologist resurfaced when Oz
Garton answered my call.

Oz and I were about the same age. We'd worked toward
bachelor degrees at separate universities during the late sixties and seventies. But unlike me, Oz continued in the
field, garnering a doctoral degree and winning an appointment as a professor of wildlife at the University of Idaho.
He was recognized as an expert on population dynamics.

His work had him speculating on the following question:
If someone turned a pack of wolves loose in Yellowstone
National Park, how many elk would they eat?

"I don't know what the model is going to say," said Oz.
"But I'll try to do it without any bias."

Oz was using computer science to come up with data
that might help settle one of the hottest wildlife issues in
the western United States during the mid-1990s: the proposed reintroduction of wolves into Yellowstone National
Park. "There's a lot of data on elk," he explained. And like-
wise, there were a lot of statistics on wolves. But relatively
little scientific information existed on wolves and elk in-
teracting.

I understood the importance of Oz's work, but the more
I talked with the professor, the more I realized that his job

wasn't nearly as adventuresome as I'd envisioned. Instead of going out into the field, poking around in the wilds, and handling critters like wolves and elk, he mostly stared into a computer screen at columns of data.

It sounded too much like being an editor.

I went home that night and reflected on the day's interview. There seemed a rightness in the divergent paths Oz and I had taken. When it comes to science, the truth is in the biology. And biology is a product of detail. Oz had an appetite for poring over data. I'm not cut out for that sort of thing.

"Most of the time, what I do is all computer based," he'd said.

Most of the time, what I do is glide past the detail in search of a story's essence, I'd told Oz.

I think we both found our niche.

— • —

Diane, on the other hand, was about to take a leave of absence from her niche.

With much trepidation, she'd yielded to my insistent prodding to start a dog kennel and we began to put the word out. Hatter Creek Kennels, with the slogan "Where Tails Always Wag," was open for business. Within less than twenty-four hours, people were calling to make reservations and dogs started arriving shortly afterward. As it turned out, there was only one other boarding kennel in Latah County, excluding veterinary clinics. The demand exceeded all expectations.

"This is great!" I exclaimed after coming home from *Tribune* work to find our little kennel full of wagging tails.

"This is a lot of work," Diane corrected.

The business turned a profit almost from day one and, although the income was modest by most standards, it was a product of Diane's unwavering commitment to make sure all those tails kept wagging. I knew this because the people, in addition to happily paying their bills, showered Diane with compliments and thanks. Even the dogs were excited to see her, knowing she always had a treat in her pocket and a pat for being "good dogs." The animals did all our advertising for us.

Some two years later, in 1993, we applied to county officials and received a conditional use permit to expand the kennel by five more runs. More dogs meant more money.

"It will be our gravy, Christmas presents, gasoline to drive to Minnesota and see relatives, clothes, whatever. We'll help you," I assured her. Heidi, and especially Greta, pitched in. We all walked dogs. Diane fielded phone calls, made appointments, cleaned kennels, and fed, spoiled, and worried about her many four-legged guests. She also retained her status as top dog among the family employees. We took pictures of our canine customers and pinned them to the wall inside the kennel.

Most of our business came from university people who traveled a lot. Even a couple of famous people left their dogs with Diane. Christina Crawford, the daughter of actress Joan Crawford and author of the best-selling book *Mommy Dearest*, boarded her elderly dogs, Prince and Princess, for a number of years. Chris Stokes, a University of Idaho graduate student and member of the Jamaican Olympic bobsled team, left his dogs with us on several occasions.

Dogs with names like Juno, Sagen, Lacey, Patience, Hooker, Daisy, Bell, and uncounted others became part of our lives. Diane walked them three times a day, fed them, cleaned up after them, combed them, and consoled those who missed their owners.

"It's all right," she told the forlorn. "It's all right. They'll be back. Here, have a cookie."

Pretty soon, Diane's identity, not just her life, was inextricably linked to the kennel business. She wore kennel coats and rubber boots four to six hours a day. The kennels were bulging and she felt a deep responsibility for all the dogs. She cared just as much about the people she met and became lasting friends with several of them.

And then, about the time I thought the dog business had a life of its own and we'd regained a measure of financial security, Diane began waking up in the mornings exhausted.

"I didn't sleep very well. I ache all over," she said. "I have another migraine. Can you walk the dogs?"

"I've got to get on the road."

"Just walk them and I'll do the rest. I'll be all right."

But with every dog that arrived, with every week and month that passed, Diane seemed all the more beaten down by the demands of the work.

"I'm just so tired. These dogs . . . I can't walk them like I used to. They pull and my shoulders, hips, and knees are so sore. I don't sleep well."

"Diane, you've got to quit complaining or you need to make a doctor appointment."

"What's a doctor going to do? They'll just tell me to slow down. But I can't stop working. We need the money."

Diane, it seemed, had taken my advice. We were indeed making more money. But she was paying a price.

— • —

Meanwhile, I feared that my own job was again in jeopardy. In 1997, the nation's big newspaper chains were actively trolling for small struggling dailies and it appeared as if the

Lewiston Morning Tribune was about to undergo another change of ownership.

Tele-Communications Inc., the nation's largest cable-television operator, had come to own the *Tribune*. But TCI wasn't really interested in good newspapering as much as profits. Steadfast in his commitment to the paper and staff, Publisher Butch Alford proposed that TCI peddle the *Tribune* and three sister newspapers back to him. TCI agreed to sell, but only on the open market, meaning that my future and that of the other *Tribune* employees was suddenly hostage to the bidding process.

"Thank God we have the kennel," I said to Diane one night as we talked about the implications.

She sighed and shook her head. "I'd really like to take a break. It's been almost ten years, night and day, weekends, holidays. I like the dogs and the people, but the work is getting to me."

"I know," I said, "but just hold on until we find out what happens with the *Tribune*, okay?"

By the late 1990s, the dog kennel business had become so integral to our lifestyle that I tended to tune out Diane's complaints. It seems insensitive now when I look back on it, but I figured some of Diane's problems were self-inflicted. She refused to do anything less than the best possible job she could. And that exacted a toll. Money aside, she took pride in seeing how happy people were to come back from vacations or business trips and find their dogs just as happy.

Finally, in 1997, she put an end to my pooh-poohing. "Look, something is wrong. I'm having too many headaches. I'm living on over-the-counter painkillers and nothing helps. I feel like I'm a hundred years old."

She went to the doctor, who ran some tests and ultimately diagnosed her as having fibromyalgia. Diane showed me the doctor's letter. She'd already done some reading and had clipped a magazine article. "Here, this explains it better than I can."

I looked at the article. "Fibromyalgia is a chronic, disabling condition that causes aching and burning pain in muscles throughout the body. It strikes both sexes at any time in life, but mostly women. . . . While patients often can hold jobs, they do so in almost constant discomfort."

I looked at Diane and asked, "Is there any treatment?"

"Yes. And one of the things is to cut down on stress."

Almost on cue, the dogs outside in the kennel erupted in barking. Another customer was arriving.

"Where's my leash? I just had it here," Diane said, scurrying around. "We'll talk about this later," she told me, locating the leash, grabbing her coat and chore boots, rushing out the front door, and pasting on a smile to greet yet another wagging tail.

CHAPTER SEVEN

Beliefs

On one of our rare vacations, we left work far behind and were riding in the family van on a much anticipated visit with my family in Minnesota. We were also about to run headlong into an ugly misconception about our home state of Idaho.

The late-June day was sunny, the van's air conditioner was fighting ninety-degree heat, and the odometer told me we were only one-third of the way to our destination. We were loaded with two kids, four dogs, and enough camping gear, it seemed, to challenge highway load restrictions.

"Where are we, Dad?" Heidi lamented.

"Still in Montana."

"Montaaaana," both girls groaned. "We hate Montana. It's too big."

"How long to Grandma's?" asked Greta.

"Oh, a long time. Two more days."

"Why don't you two try to take a nap," Diane implored as she wedged a pillow between her head and the window in an attempt to catch some sleep of her own.

"Yeah, take a nap," I said. "It will make the trip go faster."

We drove on into the expanse of eastern Montana. The words *Big Sky Country* labeled the license plates of the cars that steadily came up from behind and passed us. Within a few minutes Diane and the girls were fast asleep. I steadied our Plymouth Voyager down the freeway, content with the fifty-five-mile-an-hour pace and thinking ahead to staying in the family cabin on Roy Lake where I'd spent so much of my childhood. The van's engine droned along and all seemed so carefree and innocent.

Suddenly, in my driver's-side rearview mirror, I noticed a fast-approaching pickup truck overtaking us in the passing lane. The truck seemed to come out of nowhere and then, when it was even with the rear of our van, the driver slowed down and appeared to be inspecting something. I thought for a second that I might have a bad tire or some other kind of vehicle trouble. Then I realized he was inspecting my bumper sticker.

A couple of years earlier, I purchased a bumper sticker for the back of the van that read: *North Idaho, A State of Mind*. I liked the slogan because it spoke to the mind-set of a place far from life's freeway. We'd sported the bumper sticker everywhere we went and had even gotten several thumbs-up while cruising on vacation the previous year in southern California.

So when the pickup truck in Montana eased even with the front of our van, I looked over figuring to make eye contact with yet another person who understood the meaning of being from northern Idaho. And the guy *was* smiling. But instead of extending a friendly thumbs-up, he delivered a crisp Nazi salute. Then he sped on by.

"Did you see that?"

"What? See what?" Diane said, waking from her slumber.

"That dude in the pickup. That one right there." I pointed to the vehicle that was fast gaining speed ahead of us. "He gave me a Nazi salute."

"What? Why did he do that?" Diane asked sleepily.

"I'm not sure. . . . Maybe . . ." And then it dawned on me. In his twisted mind, the guy thought our bumper sticker spoke to his own prejudiced mind-set. He was saluting me as a comrade, a white supremacist—a damn fellow bigot.

"That does it. As soon as we get to Minnesota I'm taking the bumper sticker off."

"Do you really think that's what he meant?" asked Diane.

"I'm not sure. But I don't want anyone to even think that way about us."

I clenched the steering wheel in my hands, watched the pickup truck disappear into the distance, and looked in the rearview mirror again to see that the girls had been awakened by all the commotion.

Greta caught my eyes in the mirror, popped her thumb out of her mouth, and said, "What's a Nazi?"

— • —

Some people believe that Idaho is a haven for bigots, neo-Nazis and the so-called militia movement. I don't agree, but I concede that the belief lingers.

To believe means to give credence to an idea, sometimes without a lot of facts to support the view. I remember, for example, reciting as a boy the Apostles' Creed in church: "I believe in God the father almighty, maker of heaven and earth. . . ." Other than the first sentence in the book of Genesis and the assurance of other believers, I had no facts to support the notion. But I believed it with all my heart and soul.

Gail Hart, who answered my call one day, believed that she and her family had found a piece of paradise in Idaho— until a guy named Bo Gritz announced that he was also moving to a place known as Quaker Hill. A thirty-eight-year-old wife and mother of four children, Gail worried about reports that Gritz was a bigot and rumors that white supremacists would arrive on his heels.

"If you look right out the window, where there are new utility poles," Gail said, pointing in the direction of the Seven Devils mountain range, "that's where Bo Gritz is going to set up his community to resist the government, if necessary."

America's most decorated Vietnam Green Beret and a self-proclaimed leader of the right-wing patriot movement, Gritz said he left his home in Nevada and found nirvana when he came to Idaho. In fact, Gritz called his new building development Almost Heaven. The national media swarmed over the story, as did the *Tribune*. The belief among detractors, the media reported, was that Gritz planned to establish a militia compound, train his followers in paramilitary tactics, resist all government intervention, and foster hatred and racism.

"I believe by nineteen ninety-six you're going to see the noose tightened up around liberty's neck," Gritz growled. "For that reason, we're training people not to be paramilitary, but to live off the grid . . . so they can have a choice. We will defend our neighbors against any kind of predator threat. . . . Tyranny always wears a badge of authority."

Gail Hart prefaced her concerns about Gritz by peering out across the lush green hay fields surrounding her farmhouse and reciting some history about the community of Woodland, Idaho, otherwise known as Quaker Hill.

"In about eighteen ninety-five, twenty-six Quaker families came out here by wagon train to homestead and some of those families are still here today." For just shy of a century, said Gail, the tiny community of farmhouses had revolved around a gentle Quaker lifestyle of hard work, devotion to family, unassuming independence, and passive resistance to anything that hinted of aggression.

"Most of the people in the immediate area attend the Quaker church," she said. "When we moved here, we decided to join because we liked their ideas of gender and racial equality."

And like most people in the area, Gail had not paid much attention to Gritz until he announced that he intended to make Idaho his home. "I don't want to sound like I'm real nervous," she said, "but he admits that he prepares people in military methods to defend themselves against the government. The idea of all these gunshots going off over there is just sad."

Gritz, who ran for president in 1992 on the Populist Party ticket, gained most of his national notoriety when federal authorities grudgingly acknowledged him as being a key figure in quelling the deadly standoff with Randy Weaver and his family on infamous Ruby Ridge in northern Idaho. A hero to some, a headline grabber and bigot to others, Gritz returned to Idaho some two years later and announced plans to establish what he called a "Christian constitutional covenant community." He dubbed it Almost Heaven, and the 280-acre site was less than half a mile away from Gail Hart's farmhouse.

"I'm very worried," she said.

The juxtaposition was stark. On the one hand, the quiet Woodland community residents practiced their Quaker faith and worked the land in a place where time almost stood still. Then along came Gritz, trumpeting his politics of doom while assuring anyone willing to listen that his intentions were righteous.

Gail had trouble buying the Gritz bombast. She wanted her family to mirror the unassuming ways of the Quaker people. "They're very warm-hearted," Gail said of church members and others who lived on Quaker Hill. "They have a history of plain living." Passive resistance, not armed confrontation, she said, had long been the cornerstone of Quaker ideology, as reflected in the group's tradition of conscientious objection to war.

"We've done a certain amount of running around over the years," Gail said, and coming to Woodland seemed to be the right decision. Gail's husband, Ken, was the Lewis County agriculture extension agent and managed the family farm on the other side of Lolo Creek. The four Hart children, ranging in age from six to seventeen, attended school in Kamiah. Gail graduated from Seattle Pacific University with a bachelor's degree in piano pedagogy. She still taught lessons. She also boasted a master's degree in education from the University of Idaho.

"It's a good location for us," she said. "We like the community . . . as is."

Within a year, a smattering of people from across the United States began buying lots in the Almost Heaven development. The media literally descended on the place in helicopters. Stories were littered with unsubstantiated rumors about bunkers being built and automatic gunfire filling the air. Gritz finally arrived at Almost Heaven in early July of 1996 amid much hoopla on the hill. He stood in the bright sunshine with the open sky all around him and declared, "The road ends here for me. I'm not going anywhere but here."

To many, Gritz was a harmless windbag. But others feared that he might indeed attract a fringe element and make Idaho's reputation a self-fulfilled prophecy. Gail and her family weren't about to wait around for answers. Three months after Gritz arrived, she, Ken, and the Hart children moved to Nezperce, Idaho. Gritz, after going through a contentious divorce and attempting suicide, eventually moved back to Nevada.

— • —

For me, there's a place that represents all that is good about Idaho. It's my own "Almost Heaven." The Wild Rose Cemetery rests just south of Deary, Idaho, amid the undulating farmland of Big Bear Ridge in Latah County, surrounded by wheat fields and a panoramic view. The rest of the world seems to rise reverently up to the tiny cemetery.

The simplicity of the place keeps beckoning me back, if for no other reason than to enter the seventy-year-old cemetery chapel, play "Amazing Grace" on the old piano, and revisit my own struggles with faith.

The chapel doors are always unlocked. Besides the out-of-tune upright, the only furnishings are an altar and thirteen wooden pews. Eight vertical windows, six along the sides, two in back, fill the sanctuary with sunlight during the day and the moon and stars at night. The gravestones in the Wild Rose Cemetery date back to the late 1800s. I've twisted my way around the plots many times and contemplated the epitaphs.

"Farewell my wife and children all," reads the marker over Thomas H. Moore's grave. "From you, a father, Christ doth call."

Hanna M. McKee died in 1893 and the words on her stone read: "She was a kind, affectionate wife, a fond mother and friend to all."

Little Gertrude Emmett was born on June 5, 1892, and

died just five months later. "Budded on earth to bloom in heaven," her epitaph reads.

Once, after stopping at the cemetery and finishing yet another rendition of "Amazing Grace," I turned to leave and noticed four fresh butt prints in the dust upon one of the front pews. A quartet of sinners like me, I speculated, had paid a visit earlier in the day. Then again, I thought, perhaps some souls from out in the cemetery saw me enter and came to listen. I turned back to the piano, slowly reached out, and used one hand to play the melody of "Imagine," my favorite John Lennon song about there being no heaven or hell.

Part of me thinks I'm going to get struck by lightning when I do things like that. But for me, "Amazing Grace" and Lennon's "Imagine" speak to the spectrum of spirituality. I've even suggested, much to Diane's consternation, that the two tunes be played at my funeral.

— • —

Another old hymn that tends to haunt me is titled "Just a Closer Walk with Thee." I can still hear the melody as the pipe organ played in Saint Phillips Lutheran Church, where I attended as a boy. When my mother devoutly sang the lyrics about "gentle Jesus," I just knew the streets in heaven were lined with beautiful flowers and fountains and that the sky was blue and the breeze always balmy.

But it wasn't until after I started writing my column that I met a couple who actually *confirmed* my childhood image of heaven.

The Revs. Eldon and Ethel Bomley were husband-wife pastors at the New Life Chapel in Kamiah, Idaho. Their church, with a congregation that varied between sixty and ninety members over some two decades, was one of fifteen or more houses of God in town.

You might say Eldon Bomley, who had a license to fly small aircraft, was a sky pilot in both body and spirit. His belief in the hereafter, said Eldon, was instilled by more than Bible teachings. His wife, Ethel, claimed to have visited heaven during an out-of-body experience and hugged Jesus.

"The minute I left earth and went into Jesus' arms, it was just like this life had never been," said Ethel, who was nineteen at the time of her professed exaltation. "I just ran into his arms and I wrapped my arms around his neck and he wrapped his arms around me."

Most people believe in things that are unbelievable. It's called faith. And most religions are based on faith in a hereafter. If we knew for a fact what happens after death, whether it be a grand ascension into the clouds or a simple cessation of reality, there'd be no need to fret. Religion at that point would be devoted to mere earthly matters, like practicing the golden rule.

Of course, no one knows for sure what the grand scheme is all about. And so we all continue to believe in something unbelievable. Even those who say life simply ends are taking an unconfirmed stance.

With that kind of thinking in mind, I sat in the Bomley parsonage with Ethel and Eldon, not just listening, but eagerly probing for more insight into the hereafter. I warned them that many readers probably wouldn't believe them.

The Bomleys acknowledged my expectation by pointing out that many people don't believe the Bible when they read it. "I was brought up in a Pentecostal background and Baptist," Ethel explained. "There's been a lot of people who preach their own convictions and opinions, instead of pure Bible."

As staunch fundamentalists, Eldon and Ethel said they followed the Bible word for word with no equivocation. And that made their church something special.

"You go to a store, you like to have a lot of things to pick from," Eldon said of the world's many religions, denominations, and houses of worship. "But actually, there's only one true church . . . and that's the born again believers."

At that point, I couldn't help but think of all the non-Christian religions in the world and the billions of people (perhaps millions within the Christian faith itself) who'd take the Bomleys to task for being so exclusionary. On the other hand, a small part of me envied their dogmatic vision. It wasn't like they were trying to cram their beliefs down my throat as much as they wanted to celebrate what they'd found to be true. I wished I could be so sure about empyreal things.

Eldon, fifty-nine, was the pastor of the church. Ethel was the assistant pastor. And their ministry was indeed a partnership. They preached scripture, the Trinity, the fall of man, baptism by immersion, communion, tithing, divine healing, hell, eternal retribution, the second coming of Christ, and, of course, salvation.

"My husband has been one to preach just the Bible, nothing else," said Ethel. Both thought the world had become too consumed with materialism and ungodly ways, that people had lost sight of truth, and that sin was gaining more and more of a foothold.

"It's the TV and the newspaper and the morals . . . the lack of absolute truths. In other words, if it feels good, do it," said Eldon, offering his diagnosis of the world's ills. Then he told of how the Holy Spirit had actually been revealed to him years ago while he was making breakfast.

"All of a sudden, there was a baptism . . . and I was

speaking tongues," he said. "It wasn't something I learned; it was a language I don't understand."

The devil's advocate in me didn't consider that fair. The Bomleys had something over everybody else who had to rely on mere faith. They claimed actually to have met God. And for that, Eldon and Ethel acknowledged, they felt blessed.

"Being a Christian minister, a lot of people think you're supernatural, but you're just another human being," Ethel said.

"The only thing," added Eldon, "is that God has put a calling on us."

Ethel's calling came amid claims that she'd already visited heaven. I wanted to write about that but, again, I warned her that the story might leave readers doubting her credibility. She politely dismissed my words with the wave of a hand and resurrected the story she'd told many times before.

"When I was nineteen," she began, "I died and had an out-of-body experience." As a child, she said, she'd been placed in a foster home and suffered years of abuse. One night, after returning from a revival, she took ill.

"I just laid down and all of a sudden I could take a breath in, but not out." That's when Ethel said she felt herself rising up from her body. "I looked at myself lying there and I just felt so free. I just went right up through the ceiling."

Ethel said she'd written about her experience and had it published three times, once in the Kamiah newspaper. So it wasn't really news.

I assured her it was news to *me*.

After rising through the ceiling of her home, Ethel continued, she followed a pathway that slanted upward toward a bright light.

"All of a sudden, I realized it was Jesus," she said. "He

would just smile and . . . he'd say, 'Come,' and he showed me different parts of heaven."

I thought of the lyrics to the haunting old hymn: "Just a closer walk with thee . . ."

Ethel said she wanted to stay in heaven, but Christ said she'd someday have a husband and family and ministry to fulfill.

"He turned me around and gave me a little shove." And then she returned to her body.

Seven years after I interviewed the Bomleys, a letter came to my mailbox at the newspaper. It was from the Rev. Eldon Bomley. Ethel, he wrote, had died and been reunited with Jesus.

Good for her, I thought, folding the letter closed. I'm still not sure about the hereafter. But I truly believe that Ethel had a bead on it and died with a peaceful soul. What more could anyone ask?

— • —

No matter how religiously a faith is practiced, things happen in the world that just can't be explained through any doctrine, canon, or creed. Why, for example, Stan died and left Diane for me to find will always mystify me. And what about Heidi never knowing her real dad?

My puzzlement over God's mysterious ways increased after spending perhaps forty-five minutes interviewing Jim Chames about his career as a school administrator. At one point Jim turned to his wife, Ledley, for her input and she proudly recited the names of the couple's children and grandchildren.

And then added, "We have a little granddaughter who died."

I hesitated, but mustered the nerve to ask, How?

"She drowned."

Where?

"In the bathtub."

An accident, I thought.

"No," said Ledley, casting a hesitant glance at her husband.

I waited for the answer.

"Her mother drowned her."

I was speechless.

"Yes, her mother isn't well," Ledley continued, referring to the woman who'd married their son, Wayman Chames.

The child, fifteen-month-old Jamie Marie, was buried behind the Chames house in Peck, Idaho, up on a hill in a little grave covered with stones piled by family members.

"When the baby died, we figured the Lord knows why better than we do," said Ledley, a licensed practical nurse who'd moved to Idaho with her husband at the end of his career.

We'd talked about Jim's story for almost an hour. But now the death of this little baby seemed so much more compelling. I asked the Chameses how they could possibly deal with such a loss.

"You have to develop a philosophy to pull through a lot of stuff," said Jim, acknowledging that perhaps it was time to let people know about the grave. "Sometimes you can cope with life better if you know the facts."

The facts, at least the pertinent ones, were contained in a prosecutor's file in Oregon's Multnomah County. Jim and Ledley's daughter-in-law had been determined "unable to aid and assist" in her trial, District Attorney John Bradley told me. He declined further comment because the murder case was pending. According to Oregon newspaper reports, investigators said Jamie Marie's mother apparently thought her child was possessed by demons.

Jim, Ledley, and I walked up the hill to the grave. Standing solemnly over their granddaughter, the Chameses seemed oblivious to my presence. They just stood and looked down at the soil and stones. I clicked the camera a few times and they remained the same, not registering my invasion of what had become sacred family ground. Ledley stood with her arms folded one over the other and shivered slightly in the brisk December wind. Christmas was just around the corner and it seemed to me that celebration would be impossible, at least in the Chames family. How could God let such wicked things happen?

"You can't ask yourself why," Ledley said. She and Jim had talked on the telephone with their daughter-in-law and were convinced that the woman had no criminal intentions.

"I don't feel it's her fault," said Jim. "It wasn't like an actual, premeditated murder. We have no animosity toward the mother."

"If God can forgive you, we can," Ledley said she's told her daughter-in-law. "She doesn't know what happened." Ledley said the mother had alluded to Jamie Maire's being possessed by demons, but also about seeing a lamb in a field.

"And she said the wolf was going to get the little lamb, so she took it to give to God before the wolf could take it."

Some two years later, Jamie Marie's mother was tried for murder and convicted. Deemed insane, she was sentenced for life and placed in a mental hospital. She was released in 1990 and remains under the supervision of mental-health experts in Clackamas County, Oregon.

A headstone now rests over Jamie Marie's grave. Her father, Wayman, made it. The inscription reads: "We may make our plans, but the end results are in God's hands. Proverbs: 16."

Some twelve years after going up the hill to the grave with the Chameses, I contacted Ledley again. Jim had died of cancer two years earlier after going to California for treatments. Ledley still had her husband's ashes and was determined to grant his last wish someday.

"He told me to get a posthole digger and bury him next to Jamie, near her left side, closest to her heart, I guess," Ledley said. She'd yet to do that, but she'd indeed come to further grips with the tragedy.

"I don't hold God responsible for any of it. With Jim, I tell everyone that God takes the best. And there's a reason for taking Jamie, but I'll maybe never know it." Ledley told me the little girl had come back to her in a vision.

"Nobody believes in this stuff and they think you're crazy, but I actually saw her. . . . She was in the mirror. And I told her she was an angel now, so you go be with God. And I haven't seen her since."

As for herself, Ledley said she'd returned to Peck from California after her husband's death to pursue a "humble mission" God had suggested. "I'm going to give everyone half of my heart and a smile," she said. "I know why God left me here now, because I go and meet people and I hug them."

— • —

If there's one place I've failed miserably as a husband and father, it's in my lack of spiritual guidance and example. How can someone guide when he himself is lost? When I met Diane, she expressed her Christian beliefs with no hesitation. She also accepted what I called my fall from faith.

"It's not like I don't believe in God," I explained. "I just don't understand the mechanics of Christianity. I don't understand why God needed Jesus to die for our sins. It doesn't make any sense to me. It's all so unbelievable."

"That's where faith comes into play," said Diane.

"I know. But I just can't buy it."

Heidi was baptized into her daddy Stan's Catholic religion. Greta was baptized a Lutheran, like her mom and me. Diane was quite involved early in our marriage, teaching Sunday school and being an active member of the congregation. But after the girls were older, we didn't attend church regularly, except on Christmas and Easter, and whenever Diane could convince me that the investment of an hour on Sunday might someday result in spiritual dividends.

Christianity, like all of the world's older religions, is a relative newcomer to North America. Missionaries brought Christ's word west in the early nineteenth century. Before that, Native Americans like Nellie Axtell's relatives practiced what was called the Seven Drums Religion.

"My family was one of the lucky ones," Nellie told me when I stopped by her office after calling her on the phone. "They never steered us toward any church. We've always maintained the longhouse religion. Actually, it's not a religion. It's a way of life."

Nellie, forty-five at the time, was one of an estimated 150 full-blooded Nez Perce Indians left in the world. What's more, she was one of the few tribal members who still practiced the Seven Drums Religion. Her father, Horace Axtell, was a respected Nez Perce elder who still adhered to the "old ways."

Religions tend to be practiced both internally and externally. I was raised a Lutheran and learned that the key to salvation was simply having an inner faith that Jesus Christ was my savior. All the good deeds in the world wouldn't get me into heaven if I didn't accept the underlying truth that

Jesus died for my sins. And at one time in my life, I embraced that concept wholeheartedly. I had faith. But I also wondered why it was necessary to jump through so many spiritual hoops, like attending Sunday services, Bible lessons, and other church functions. My Catholic friends seemed even more demonstrative about their faith. Just what was the difference between *being* religious and *practicing* a religion? Was one dependent on the other? Or could a good Lutheran get to heaven without going to church?

Nellie, even though she claimed to have been "spared" the teachings of Christianity, offered some insights.

"Every day when I was a little girl, my grandmother would say, 'You have to do it this way.' It still rings in my ears," said Nellie of the childhood teachings passed down through the generations. When the missionaries came on the heels of the Lewis and Clark Expedition, Nellie explained, tribal children were taught to deny many of the old ways. They were even whipped for speaking their native tongue. But through what I assume was nothing less than unflinching determination, families like Nellie's resisted. English, she said, was kept a second language in her household and the traditional ways became embedded in her heart.

"Now it's time for me to take a step forward, instead of backwards, and become an elder," she declared. At the time we talked, Nellie was working as an administrative assistant in the tribal fisheries program. She spent most of her days at a computer screen. But for several weeks during the spring of each year, Nellie stepped away from technology and back in time.

"Generally, there are seven women. We've been digging. A lot of times, you'll see me alone," said Nellie. The Nez Perces, like most indigenous peoples, were hunters and gatherers. The digging of which Nellie spoke in such reverent tones was the traditional unearthing of roots that tribal members had done for generations.

"*Camas, komstit, kouse,*" said Nellie, reciting the earth's offerings. And there was *kaa-keet,* a root afforded special attention in the spring. "The women who go dig have to sweat and perform ceremonies for seven days." A traditional root feast would include various roots as well as wild game like salmon, elk, and deer.

"It's like a birthday for Mother Earth, the beginning of another cycle," said Nellie. The earth could be disturbed, according to Nez Perce teachings, for only two reasons: when digging for roots and when burying the dead.

Nellie bemoaned the way the Nez Perce people had been swallowed by Western civilization and become so focused on moneymaking ventures like building bingo halls and casinos. She and the others who clung to the Seven Drums way of life thought it was more important to build a longhouse where their religious beliefs could be practiced. The tribe's last longhouse, which had been adjacent to the Clearwater River, was ripped from its foundation in 1975 by a spring flood.

"We're really losing our identity fast," said Nellie. Unless her people resumed their ancient practices, their spiritual taproot would decay and be reclaimed by the earth. The only way to stay in touch with the old ways, she said, was to keep digging and sweating and practicing the traditional teachings.

Perhaps that was *my* problem, I thought. Maybe I'd lost my religious identity because I was out of practice. I couldn't remember the last time I took communion or really prayed the way I was taught to pray as a child.

Five years after Nellie Axtell introduced me to the Seven Drums Religion, her father, Horace, passed along good news. The tribe had agreed to build a longhouse on a hill near Sweetwater, Idaho, upstream a couple of miles along Lapwai Creek from where the old longhouse once stood.

Said Horace, "The elders told us: 'Never let go of spirituality.' Hopefully, what we're doing will bring spirituality to our young people and the newborns."

Could it be, I asked myself, that my own spiritual floundering was a product of gradually retreating from what I'd been taught: to attend church, study the Bible, pray, and otherwise live my faith?

There are some people, of course, who'll tell you it's easier to connect with divinity and "the larger scheme of things" contemplating nature than sitting on a church pew. I guess I've always shied in the former direction. Which is why, when I interviewed fishermen like Jake Guhlke and Howard Monk for my column, I detected something supernal in their chosen hobby. Perhaps unconsciously my mind was casting back to the opening pages of Norman MacLean's novel *A River Runs Through It*, which testify to the religious power of fishing in the Northwest.

"In our family," wrote MacLean, "there was no clear line between religion and fly fishing. We lived at the junction of great trout rivers in western Montana, and our father was a Presbyterian minister and fly fisherman who tied his own flies and taught others. He told us about Christ's disciples being fishermen, and we were left to assume, as my brother and I did, that all first-class fishermen on the Sea of Galilee were fly fisherman, and that John, the favorite, was a dry fly fisherman."

Jake and Howard were anglers who could embrace MacLean's prose, but appreciated angling in different ways. Jake liked fishing. Howard liked catching. And within those two approaches, I figure, lie the mysteries of why some people turn to water to renew their belief in a higher power.

"Every river holds ten thousand secrets," Jake said. "You unlock those secrets with experience and skill." Jake wasn't the kind of man who'd fish and tell. But like Norman MacLean, he'd seduce you with talk of rivers, lakes, and lunkers. And if you were really lucky, he might even show you his late father's bamboo fly rod—maybe even let you hold it.

I got lucky.

Almost reverently, Jake pulled the four-piece rod from its cloth case. Then he assembled the sections, slowly and precisely, like no more precious treasure existed on earth. And finally he placed the rod in my hands.

"That was his rod and you didn't use it," said Jake, recalling the childhood law by which he still abided. Resisting the urge to feign a cast, I simply held the work of art a moment longer before returning it to its owner.

"What we have today is way ahead of bamboo," Jack observed. He set aside his father's old rod and pulled out a custom-made graphite model with gold inlays.

"It just adds pleasure to what you're doing," said Jake, justifying the extras he'd added when building the rod. "It's like driving a Cadillac."

About forty miles back into the mountains from where Jake showed me his souped-up fly rod, sixty-one-year-old Howard Monk cruised Elk Creek Reservoir aboard a pontoon boat. Among the ranks of trout fishermen, Howard was the antithesis of Jake Guhlke. Whereas Jake epitomized deft casting, refined fly tying, and the never-ending pursuit of knowledge about aquatic life-forms, Howard was a "catch-and-keep" kind of guy.

"I just love to fish," proclaimed Howard. "And I very seldom go out and don't get my limit."

Sporting the scars of recent bypass heart surgery, Howard said fishing was good not only for his health, but also for his outlook on life. There are only so many fishing days in a life, he reasoned, so you better take advantage of them all.

— • —

While there are many religions within the *Lewiston Tribune*'s circulation area, they're practiced against a relatively colorless ethnic backdrop. Unlike other parts of America, the region never became a racial melting pot. Even on the campuses of the University of Idaho, Washington State University, and Lewis-Clark State College, recruitment of minority students hasn't really changed the overall complexion. In this part of the country diversity remains more a goal than a reality.

Take Kellie Richardson, for instance. An aspiring broadcast journalist, she was an eighteen-year-old communications major matriculating at Washington State University in Pullman. When I interviewed her, she spoke not of working sensational stories that might make national headlines, but of exposing simmering stereotypes.

"I don't really like to talk about the way things should be," said Kellie, who was from Tacoma, Washington. So she sat me down to explain in no uncertain terms the way things *were* for a young black woman in a world surrounded by wheat fields, white faces, and ignorance.

"I came here and people would ask me the strangest things. They automatically thought I was on an athletic scholarship." One day, for example, she remarked in the company of strangers that she was tired. Several people assumed she'd been running laps for track. But she'd simply stayed up late studying.

"I speak. I write and I read," said Kellie. "And I'm black. That's my thing."

In fact, she was attending WSU on an academic scholarship.

"I know. It's hard to believe, but I try to be patient."

I really had no idea what it was like for Kellie. Not only was I almost three times her age, I'd never experienced what it was like to be in a minority. I grew up in a Minneapolis suburb and can't remember a black student in school. That changed when I attended the University of Minnesota and lived off-campus in a St. Paul neighborhood. Upon moving west, however, I was back in the majority.

Even today, I doubt if there are more than a dozen black families living within the *Tribune's* circulation area—excepting those in the university towns of Moscow and Pullman. Kellie suggested, though, that there was an upside to the lack of racial variety. "I find that a lot of people from rural areas are more open than people from Tacoma." News coverage in her hometown, for example, focused too much on blacks and crime. "I've yet to see anything really positive when I'm watching the news," she said. "Unless we [blacks] make a touchdown. Then we make the front page."

As for the WSU campus, Kellie said it was more a reflection of the bigger cities and that officials needed to wake up. "The administration really pisses me off," she said, claiming that too many people were paying little more than lip service to the many problems that existed, including the subtle prejudices against minorities that are sometimes worse than overt racism. "It's not so much that they need to do something as that they should acknowledge minority students have something worthwhile to say."

Kellie believed that, even among white women on campus, there were gross misunderstandings about black women. "I talk when given a chance," she said. "But white women seem afraid they're going to say something and that I'm going to go off."

The bottom line, said Kellie, is that there are no politically correct ways to be blunt. Candid discussion, no matter how uncomfortable, is the key to shedding stereotypes.

"Deal with it," she said. "That's my thing."

Kellie eventually changed her major from communications to psychology and graduated from WSU in 1998. By the time she got her degree, she said WSU had made great strides in encouraging diversity among its student body, staff, faculty, and administration. "At WSU for a while, it was just rhetoric. Now they're doing it."

But off campus and back in the real world, Kellie told me there was still much work to be done. When we talked again, she was twenty-three, had a two-year-old daughter, and had just started working at Pacific Lutheran University in Washington as a student recruiter and adviser. And yes, she was still telling it like it is:

"I think tension is good. Someone being out of their comfort zone, that's good for you." The world wouldn't, couldn't, and shouldn't ever be color blind, she insisted. Putting racism behind us, she suggested, smacks of Pollyannaish thinking. The bigots must be kept square in the sights, she said.

"Besides, it's all subtle now. A lot of racism is really institutionalized now. There's a very racist kind of power structure that keeps people marginalized. I think a lot of people fear the unknown."

Kellie said she continued to write about racism, if for no other reason than to vent. She shared a piece titled "Tales from the Dark(er) Side." I think she wanted to make sure I wouldn't get too comfortable, or, worse, go color blind. She wrote the following about what she called black rage:

Not until I entered the work world did I fully participate in the legacy of slavery and oppression. Never had my hair felt kinkier, never had my skin felt darker, never had my hips felt rounder, never had my lips felt fuller, never had my spirit felt weaker. . . . I must find my gift to the world, just as you must. It's at this point, however, that I realize how difficult and gut wrenching that can be when you're not White. But I've never been afraid of the dark, and I ain't about to start now.

Kellie's story in mind, I recall a high school basketball game between the Lapwai Wildcats and the Potlatch Loggers. Entrance to the state championship was at stake.

Lapwai is where the headquarters of the Nez Perce Tribe are located. Potlatch was founded as a logging community in the early 1900s. Diane and both of our daughters attended school in Potlatch.

Greta was in junior high school when she became an avid Logger fan. We went to most of the games. I kept score and taught her what I knew about the beauty of the sport. She learned about the intensity of the Potlatch-Lapwai rivalry by herself. Whenever the teams met, the boys on both teams were unrelenting in their quest for victory. Whispers also circulated about the game pitting the "rednecks" from Potlatch against the "red skins" from the reservation.

On this night, Potlatch prevailed by a handful of points. It had been a hard-fought clash and players on both teams seemed to accept the outcome with genuine handshakes and a show of mutual respect. In fact, the two teams had become so evenly matched over the previous few years that fans on both sides graciously accepted their victories, knowing full well it might be different at the next meeting.

But this was the last game of the season for the loser.

And my daughter was about to experience firsthand the sting of racial slurs and prejudice. Surrounded by other happy Potlatch fans, we left the gymnasium in Lewiston, then took the sidewalk toward our car. The February night was cold, and just before we reached our vehicle, another car came racing up the street. It was filled with young Lapwai fans. When they saw us wearing Potlatch green, the windows came down and the words spilled out that still thunder in my head.

"F—— you, you white motherf——ers," a young man screamed as the car sped past.

I'd like to say I was saddened by the incident because it was so typical of the racism that continues to saturate American society. But I wasn't sad. I was enraged. I was angry for my daughter. She didn't deserve to be the target of such abusive language. She had, in fact, taken a childhood interest in Native American culture, especially the Nez Perces' historic links to the Appaloosa horse. She treasured, for example, a picture of Nez Perce horseman Jackson Sundown. The picture, which had been given to her by Bill Picard of the tribe's executive committee, still hangs in Greta's bedroom.

But then I realized, as peculiar as it may sound, that it was nothing personal. We were simply random targets absorbing yet another volley of bigotry that could have gone either way. I put my arms around Greta as she stood dumbfounded on the sidewalk. I knew that what she'd just experienced probably paled in comparison to the kind of verbal abuse young Nez Perce children had endured. Still, my heart went out to her.

"What did I do?" she asked.

"Nothing," I assured. "They just lost the game."

Of course, it was much more than a game that generated those words. Perhaps that's why I'm still angry all these years later—not because those young people got away with their insult, but because it *was* so impersonal. They didn't know us and we didn't know them. Surely, if we'd encountered one another face-to-face, the communication would have been less contentious.

— • —

J. Herman Reuben, a Nez Perce tribal elder whom I interviewed for the column, used the example of a legendary animal to explain the wonders of spirituality, the unsettling nature of racism, and other dynamics at work in what he called the circle of life.

At sixty-five years old, Herman had held a number of jobs, including chairman of the tribe's executive committee. But it was another job title, that of "storyteller," that he found himself embracing most heartily. He felt an urgency to focus more and more on the old days when tribal elders told him stories. By passing the tales along to young people, both Indians and non-Indians, Herman said he hoped to help his heritage survive.

"Like Coyote survived," said Herman. "He was kind of an all-around guy."

Coyotes are my favorite animals because they continue to prevail in the face of so much prejudice and discrimination. Western civilization has spent the better part of two centuries trying to eradicate the song dogs. But they continue to sing in the night. They are wily by nature and are survivors by virtue of their tenacity. Unlike their more powerful cousins, wolves, which have wrestled with extinction, coyotes have frolicked in the face of intolerance.

Diane, the girls, and I have watched coyotes from our home on Hatter Creek as they nudge through the tall grass in search of mice, pouncing like playful puppies on the hunt. When they sing from the woods, we always hush one another and say, "Listen. Do you hear them?"

Herman explained that "Coyote had the assignment of protecting his people and letting human beings know they had to respect the animals." Before Christianity came west, the Nez Perce religion was firmly established in nature. To understand the Nez Perces as a people, he suggested, you might rely on Coyote.

"We have to teach the non-Indian how we view the natural environment," Herman reasoned. "Coyote is a survivor. He survived thousands of years. Today's Indian has had to learn to be a survivor."

Herman frequently visited with children in the schools, teaching them how to make the sign of Coyote with their hands and sharing his childhood memories.

"I begin by telling them about the tepee," said Herman "and how we lived in the mountains and how, when night came, I'd snuggle up to my grandmother and say, 'Tell me a story about Coyote.' "

The stories always began the same way. "My grandmother, she'd say, 'Once upon a time, Coyote was going upriver.' He was always going up the river."

I told Herman about my own experiences with coyotes, including one time in June when we awoke to the bleating of a small fawn near the edge of the woods. We watched as the mother deer tried to defend her offspring. The coyote seemed to be toying with the deer. He'd chase the fawn until the doe flew at him with her sharp front feet. Then the coyote would stop, sit, and pant, with what appeared to be a sly grin on his face. Eventually the doe prevailed and the little fawn slipped away down the draw.

"Coyote was playing, not hunting," said Herman.

But about two hours later, Greta, who was six at the time, looked out the front window to see the coyote again, slinking its way down the same draw, nose alternately to the ground and to the wind in search of the fawn.

"No, no, no," screamed Greta. And she was gone—flying off the porch and running across the hay field with her arms waving. The coyote saw her coming, stopped dead in his tracks, turned tail, and ran off.

"Aaah," Herman said. "You see, Coyote taught your daughter on that day how to be brave."

A photograph of a coyote hung in Herman's office. The animal in the picture seemed to be overseeing his work. It was appropriate, said Herman, because Coyote continued to assume a more important role in where his own life was leading.

"There is a circle of life," he explained. "We believe that we're part of the Mother Earth. We never did consider owning the land." That's why, he said, Coyote continues to jump fences, travel over mountains, ford streams, and defy attempts by humans to kill his kind.

"He's always going upriver against the current. That's what survivors do."

Less than two months after we talked, Herman suffered a massive heart attack and died at Saint Joseph Regional Medical Center—downstream from his home at Lapwai.

— • —

I've long been beguiled by death. Not out of some macabre fixation, but simply because mortality is such a common denominator. To really live life to its fullest, it seems only logical that one must first come to grips with death.

On my most recent stop at the Wild Rose Cemetery, the chapel doors were thrown wide open, the pews were gone, and the walls and ceiling sported a fresh layer of paint.

"They're refinishing the pews," said latex-spattered Kari

Galloway. She and her friend Tutti Sandmeyer were working with brush and roller to refurbish the old chapel.

"An anonymous donor is paying to have the inside painted," added Kari. The two women, both from nearby Kendrick, had been working for the better part of two weeks. They had the front and back doors propped open so the wind could coax the paint fumes out of the chapel.

"Sometimes I stop here and play the old piano."

"Oh, it's been here forever," said Tutti.

We all ambled over to the upright and I plinked a few notes.

The chapel, said Kari, was built in 1929 with lumber salvaged from the old United Brethren Church that used to stand toward the west, where nothing but rolling grain fields, some fingers of timber, and a couple distant farmhouses could now be seen. You could argue that God himself had chosen the location.

"Well," I said after talking a few minutes longer, "I think I'll go take a walk in the cemetery."

"Half my family is buried out there," said Kari.

The harvest season was in full swing and the grass around the graves was brown. The brittle blades crunched beneath my feet. A rusted iron fence cordoned off the oldest part of the cemetery. Barbed wire surrounded the perimeter of the property. I noticed that most of the newer graves were marked with flat stones, so as to make mowing easier in these fast-paced times.

The view, as always, was spectacular, even though it was clouded by a smoky haze from faraway grass or forest fires. The breeze ruffled the pages in my notebook as I jotted down my thoughts and a few epitaphs from the graves.

". . . how sweet the sound . . . that saved a wretch like me."

I walked away thinking about how John Lennon would

have sounded singing the lyrics to such a hymn. I wondered where he'd gone after he passed on and whether I'd ever have time to figure it all out—or maybe get the faith back.

Funny thing is, sometimes life doesn't give you the luxury of time. Sometimes our beliefs, spiritual or otherwise, are tested, and decisions, no matter how untimely, must be made.

CHAPTER EIGHT

Resilience

In sickness and in health, until death do us part."

The words seemed to reinvent themselves as Diane told me about the pending medical test and what it might mean for our future.

"They're going to test Mama and . . . if she has it, if it comes back positive, well, there's a fifty-fifty chance I'll test positive too."

"Would you take the test? I mean, do we really want to know?"

"I think I do," said Diane. "I think I need to know."

Throughout the mid-1980s and into the late 1990s, Diane's mother gradually deteriorated until she could no longer take care of herself. She moved from one group care facility to another and finally into the behavioral unit of a nursing home. Years of diagnosis failed to explain her condition to anyone's satisfaction. Most of the speculation among doctors, however, focused on a devastating illness called Huntington's disease. Folk singer Woody Guthrie died of the affliction. Researchers described it as an incurable combination of Parkinson's and Alzheimer's diseases.

Even if Alice tested positive, there was little that could be done. That knowledge would merely confirm what we feared.

And sure enough, several weeks after the genetic test was conducted, the worst was realized. Diane's mother tested positive for Huntington's disease.

"What's this mean?"

"It means I'm at risk. And so are Heidi and Greta.

"It means," Diane said almost matter-of-factly, "that I have to make a decision."

It also meant that I, after nearly two decades of marriage, needed to look inward. Diane was already reeling from her constant battle with fibromyalgia. And now the latest news had set a time bomb in the midst of our life.

"We'll be all right," I assured her. "We'll get through this. Remember, we made a vow to each other."

"But you didn't bargain for this, David. Neither did I. What if I turn out like Mama? I feel so bad for her."

Diane's words seemed to be echoing back from when we first met. She wasn't afraid in the sense that we all harbor concern about emulating some of the things we don't like about our parents. Diane had always suspected that there was some unseen malady that would rob her mother of life before she actually died.

"What will we do if I get tested and it turns out bad?"

"Well, I guess we have to pray that doesn't happen."

The words sounded so hypocritical coming from my mouth. I hadn't prayed in years, especially for something so important.

With the bad news, Alice's progressive decline suddenly made sense. The physical manifestations of the disease had left her in constant search of balance and prone to injury from falling. Her mind slipped among lucidity, anxiousness, and paranoia. Medication was prescribed, but she often refused treatment for fear that the medicine would make her even sicker.

I'd never really understood such obstinacy. How could someone refuse help and contribute to her own demise? And then I remembered John F. Starr. Some ten years before Diane's mother was diagnosed, John and I talked about how disquieting mental illness can be for victims and loved ones alike.

"I feel sorry for her sometimes, having to put up with me," said John, who was seventy-four when I interviewed him.

"Well, it's just one of those things, Daddy," said John's wife, Bonnie. "You didn't ask for it."

John was born and raised in the country around Southwick, Idaho, and spent most of his working days sawing timber. Now, he admitted, he spent most of his time trying to remember little things, like how to get home after walking to the mailbox.

"I get lost," he confided.

I stopped writing and tried to really listen. At such times, I've often wondered why people invite me into their lives. As the Starrs' story about Alzheimer's disease unfolded, Bonnie sometimes fought back tears while John, always smiling, tried his best to recall better days.

"I'll tell you something I remembered for a long time, when they brought the CCC [Civilian Conservation Corps] boys here from around Chicago," said John, reminiscing about the Great Depression and hard times. And then he suddenly stopped talking, as if patiently waiting for another question that might wrench up another memory from the abyss. But my next query was for Bonnie.

I wasn't sure about what the Starrs expected from me. I explained that I'd called in hope of writing their story and we could handle it one of two ways. We could dwell on the past, skirt the present, and offer a pleasant, however incomplete, biography of a marriage that had endured for fifty-three years.

Or we could share the kind of reality more and more families must endure these days.

"Well, Daddy, what do you think?" Bonnie implored.

John nodded and looked down with a smile at my pen and notebook. "It's all right."

Alzheimer's disease, which was first recognized around 1906, slowly unravels the mind and, unless death intervenes, can return an adult to infant-like dependence. According to the Alzheimer's Association and the National Institute on Aging, nearly 70 percent of all sufferers live at home with spouses or family members tending to their needs.

"I think he's happier at home than he'd be any other place," Bonnie said.

"I'll say so," John agreed.

The trouble, of course, was that John didn't always know where home was. And the problems were becoming more difficult.

"It can get kind of hectic," Bonnie said. "I can't let him go for a walk anymore because he'll get lost."

John had been to a number of doctors and undergone tests in the hospital. He was on medication and the prognosis was at best uncertain. Despite all that, the Starrs had just celebrated their fifty-third wedding anniversary without much of a hitch.

"He took me out for dinner that day," Bonnie said.

"I can't remember exactly where," he said.

"I can't either," said Bonnie, laughing. "It was that new hamburger place downtown," but she couldn't summon the name.

Funny thing, I knew what place they meant, but I

couldn't remember the name either. We all laughed at our collective forgetfulness. But when John gave me a whimsical little smile and shrugged his shoulders, I realized how trivial my momentary loss of memory was compared to the void he was experiencing.

Despite her husband's condition, Bonnie was determined to lead as active a life as possible. She drove everywhere and the two went to senior citizen meetings, visited their four children who lived in the area, went shopping, and watched their grandchildren and great-grandchildren grow up. The Starrs met near Southwick as teenagers and had lived in the area all their lives. Before retiring, John worked in the woods and then some eleven years at the Jaype plywood mill near Pierce.

"I suppose she told you I worked in the woods," John said, his long-term memory suddenly serving him well. Bonnie might have mentioned it, but I wanted to hear the story from John. I told him I loved to hear real lumberjacks talk about their work. And with that invitation, he spent the next several minutes reciting a monologue about crosscut saw days and the falling of big timber: "white pines six feet across on the stump."

"He can remember long ago," Bonnie said. "But he can't remember yesterday sometimes."

John nodded and smiled again. I remembered reading that in the advanced stages of Alzheimer's a person's vocabulary drops to six words or less, and they can't walk, sit up, or even smile. If John knew the symptoms, he seemed determined to make the best of his smile before he couldn't. When it finally came time for me to leave, I thanked the Starrs for being so candid. Maybe their story, I said, would help others know they're not alone.

"Well, that would be fine," John said.

Then Bonnie took her husband's hand, rubbed his palm, and said lovingly, "Cold hands, warm heart."

John and Bonnie lived together for about three more years before another decision had to be made. "He always said he was going home," said Bonnie, recalling how John continued to walk away, sometimes going so far that authorities had to search for him. "Sometimes he said he was going to Southwick, or up to Pierce."

Eventually, John became a resident at a local rest home. "I think he lived about seven years after you visited with us," said Bonnie when I talked to her again on the phone. "He didn't know me or anyone else. It's awful hard to see somebody get that way."

Bonnie had also moved to a care home in Lewiston after diabetes took its toll and she started losing her vision. Thankfully, she said, she had nothing but fond memories about her husband, even though failing health eventually robbed them of each other.

"I sure do miss him."

— • —

Before the diagnosis, Huntington's disease had already robbed Alice and Diane of so much. When we visited the nursing home, I watched these two women interact and the image left me looking soberly into the future.

Diane was forced to hold Alice upright in bed, snuggling her close for support. As they clung to each other, Alice sometimes flailed with uncontrollable dance-like movements known as chorea. Diane read her mother's most recent cards and letters from relatives out loud and combed Alice's hair. She tried to visit around lunch so she could feed her mother, one painful spoonful at a time, encouraging the woman who once nurtured her to "eat one more bite, Mama. Just one more."

Sometimes I had to leave the room.

In addition to limiting Alice's physical and mental abilities, Huntington's had taken away Diane's peace of mind. But I was blindly determined not to let the disease rob our family of any more.

"We'll just cope, somehow. Besides, there's a chance, a fifty-fifty chance, that you're fine."

"I hope so," said Diane. "I hope for me and you, but especially for Heidi and Greta."

"And I'll take care of you. Don't worry. If you get sick, I'll be there for you."

— • —

Patrick O'Toole's wife was there for him. In fact, his chances for survival repeatedly hung on her timely intervention. That's why on the day I visited the O'Tooles in the little farming town of Colton, Washington, Patrick had just finished cleaning the entire house. It was his way of thanking Janice for saving his life again during the night.

"It's very scary," said Janice, who explained how she had to inject a dose of glucose into her husband, lest he die. Patrick had diabetes. When his blood sugar dropped below certain levels, he slipped into a coma. It happened about once a month.

Resigned to coping with Patrick's illness for the rest of their lives together, the O'Tooles tried to lighten the deadly seriousness of the situation. They made a pact that every time Janice saved his life, Patrick would do something just as nice in return—thus the housecleaning in time for Thanksgiving Day company.

"One time," Janice told me, beaming, "he planned a romantic evening for us."

Diabetes is said to be the seventh leading cause of death in the United States. Not wanting to become a statistic, Patrick had taken to setting his alarm clock every night so he could wake on his own and check his blood-sugar level, thereby giving Janice a better night's sleep. If he didn't wake to the alarm, said Janice, she became Patrick's last line of defense.

As all-consuming as that scenario seemed, diabetes was really little more than the hub around which the O'Tooles had fashioned a lifestyle dedicated to demanding careers, a house full of pets, and, yes, someday a family.

"These guys are our children right now," said Patrick, introducing Seth the yellow Labrador, Tyler the shelty, a cat named Ying (Yang got run over), and two doves who lived in a glass aviary. Patrick was working on his doctoral degree at Washington State University in psychology and counseling. Janice was director of Opportunities Unlimited, a Moscow, Idaho–based organization dedicated to helping developmentally disabled people.

His bout with diabetes, said Patrick, had been waged since childhood. And the disease continued to remind him of just how important things like community, careers, family, and loving relationships really are. Janice felt similarly, pointing out that the only area where they diverged was that she preferred staying up late, while Patrick turned in around eight o'clock each night.

"And I always set my alarm clock," he said.

I began to think more about taking care of Diane the way the caregivers in the nursing home tended to her mother. It was a demanding task and Diane had often said she wouldn't wish her needs on anyone, especially me.

"Who knows," she ventured, trying to remain optimistic, "maybe there will be a medical breakthrough."

When I touched base with the O'Tooles a few years later, Patrick was still setting his alarm clock, but with less urgency. In fact, Janice said she couldn't really remember the last time she'd saved Patrick's life. He was now wearing a beeper-size pump connected to a tube and needle inserted into his body. The pump injected insulin into his system at a regular rate around the clock.

"It's changed our lives dramatically," said Janice.

And there was more good news. "We're seven months pregnant," Janice reported.

When I wake at night next to Diane, turn over, and see the time digitally displayed on our alarm clock, Patrick sometimes enters my mind. I can't help thinking how wonderful it must be for him to wake up and go back to sleep without a worry.

— • —

Not everyone, of course, has the great fortune of a life-saving support system, whether it's flesh and blood or mechanical.

Tom Tillson had to save himself.

He'd become the town drunk. He was the brunt of jokes, the subject of gossip, and the cause of his own dissolution. While he craved the next drink, his body trembled from the thirst.

"I'd get to where I'd have to drink a six-pack just to get rid of the shakes," admitted Tom after I called and asked him for his story. His marriage ended in divorce. Eventually, he was out of work.

"Drinking ruined my career in the woods," he confided.

Born and raised in the remote timber town of Elk River,

Idaho, Tom said he started drinking as a young teen. "We'd just get somebody to buy it for us." At the age of sixteen he moved to Moscow, Idaho, and attended school there, but never graduated. He decided to go to work instead.

"And I just continued to drink," he said.

On the day I talked with Tom, we both were drinking coffee. Across the street from the unassuming home where he lived alone was the bar he intended to buy. I gently pointed out the craziness of a recovering alcoholic's buying a bar.

"I suppose." Tom shrugged. Conveniently, the place was already called Tom's Tavern and had long been a watering hole around which much of the old logging town's nightlife revolved. During one of those fuzzy nights at the bar, Tom recalled, somebody had encouraged him to run for mayor.

"So I did, as a joke." He even got a few votes, over which the bar patrons got a few laughs. But in retrospect, Tom concluded, people were probably laughing *at* him more than *with* him. The drinking continued and finally he decided to seek help. He enrolled in a recovery unit in Spokane, Washington. But the taste of an institution, he said, was enough to drive him back to drinking.

"So I just came home and did it [kicked drinking] on my own. The tavern, that's the first place I went when I got back. I sat down and had a pop [soda]. And within a week, I was back to work."

I've met other alcoholics. I've even done a story about the "drunk tank" at State Hospital North in Orofino, Idaho, during the holiday season. I watched people writhing with delirium tremors as they went through withdrawal. Some of them hallucinated. One man cried as he tried to pull imaginary snakes off his arms. I've also had friends who've received tickets and spent time in jail for driving while intoxicated. And it's a fact that most violent crimes are somehow associated with the consumption of alcohol. Most real drunks agree that few in their ranks simply go cold turkey.

But Tom insisted that that's exactly what he did. And then, of all things, Tom's newfound sobriety steered him back into the political arena—not as a joke, but as a legitimate candidate in a three-way race. During the campaign he talked not only about issues, but about his reformation.

"People knew I'd quit. They talked me into running and I won. I guess I got about fifty percent of the vote."

Two years after we drank coffee together, Tom was still wielding the mayor's gavel. He was also the local fire chief and the head of the area recreation district.

"It will be seven years this month," he said of his sobriety. And as for the tavern, he's owned it for two years now, and he always has a cup of coffee or pop nearby. "A lot of people ask me what I'm drinking, but they know what it is."

I wondered if the key to Tom's turning the corner was literally surrounding himself with temptation. Perhaps by owning the bar and associating with others who might well be alcoholics he was able to keep his nemesis in sight and therefore at bay. But Tom preferred to think it was simply a matter of recognizing one's priorities.

Once a person is consumed by drinking, he said, he thinks short-term. He thinks about his next drink and he mulls over the next time he plans to get a handle on the behavior. Sooner or later, he either drinks himself into a stupor or he turns for help.

"When I finally decided it was time to quit, I came home and realized I was losing my friends and stuff and I just said, 'I've had enough.' That's when I started drinking pop and coffee."

In addition to making a go of the tavern and considering

a second run for mayor, Tom had also gotten married. The town planned a party of sorts, so he and his fiancée, Dawn, slipped off to Boise.

Married, mayor, recovering—no vices at all?

"Oh yes," said Tom. "I've chewed snoose for years. I'm down to two cans a week, but I can't quit."

— • —

My high school football coach once made me sit down in the locker room after a bad day on the practice field to memorize a slogan that has remained indelibly etched in my mind.

"Determination is the quality found in all great athletes that allows them to live with and overcome pain and sacrifice."

If there's a truth in that maxim, Maggi Sullivan of Clarkston, Washington, would have made a great nose tackle for the Pittsburgh Steelers. "If there's a hell," she declared, "I've been there. I really think so."

When I met Maggi, she was mixing it up with cancer and the struggle was going into overtime.

"I love life," she explained. "I feel good. And if I don't feel good, I don't let very many people know it."

Maggi's battle started with the frightening discovery of a lump in her left groin. After a series of tests, she met with her doctor.

" 'You know what I'm going to tell you,' " said Maggi, reciting the doctor's ominous greeting.

"Yes," she said. "I know. It's cancer."

It's one of those words that can rip away a person's hope. But not Maggi's. She remembered the next meeting with her doctor.

"You know why you're here?" said the physician.

"Yes, I do," answered Maggi. "I'm here to get well and you're going to help me."

Thus began Maggi's all-out blitz on the disease that was attacking her.

"Lymphoma," she said, echoing the diagnosis. "Low-grade, slow, and progressive. A five-year survival rate."

Then she talked about the hell.

"I had no control over vomiting or my bowels," said Maggi, recalling the weeks upon weeks she'd spent in hospitals over the previous ten years, writhing with the pain of chemotherapy and radiation treatments. The regimen made her go bald three different times. She endured a bone-marrow transplant and took drugs that, short of death, bludgeoned her body perhaps more than the disease itself.

"At one point, I was vomiting blood and slime. I thought I was dying. I was almost hysterical." Maggi, who was fifty-six years old when we talked, had gone in and out of remission so many times doctors called her Wonder Woman.

"They'd wonder what I was going to do next."

I asked Maggi about her goals at that point.

"To live," she said as if I were a bit thickheaded. "I just tried to be strong. I'd say, This isn't going to get me. I'm going to get it."

When she was first diagnosed, Maggi was working as an in-home beautician and sold Avon products. "I used to tell everybody, 'I'm a street walker and a door knocker.'" She was also in the midst of a divorce and her world seemed to be unraveling. But once she accepted the diagnosis, she was determined to have a say in not just the treatment, but the prognosis. She asked question upon question and demanded answers from her doctors.

When treatments seemed to fail, she demanded a referral to experts at the University of Washington. There, she qualified for an experimental bone-marrow transplant. Doctors, however, ultimately determined that her lungs weren't strong enough to survive the introduction of radioactive iodine into her system. So, as Maggi described it, she had an "old-fashioned" bone-marrow transplant. The doctors and other medical staff who treated her in Seattle endured the disease with her, establishing a special bond.

"It's terrible to say this," she said, chuckling, "but I had a lot of fun over there. I really did."

At that point, Maggi went uncharacteristically silent and tears welled up in her eyes. Then she sighed, as if tenacity alone couldn't ensure her future. "I guess it's kind of like being reborn," she explained. "I wear my angel on my shoulder every day. I'm not ready, and the man upstairs knows I'm not ready."

The cancer finally won on June 6, 1998. Maggi died at Saint Joseph Regional Medical Center in Lewiston. She was sixty.

— • —

I have a selfish wish that my sister could have fought as long as Maggi, especially when I recall that day I flew urgently back to Minnesota and gathered solemnly with my family outside the hospital room door. I remember knocking, walking in alone, and finding Maryanne bedridden and softly crying.

"Oh David, I didn't make it," she said, conceding that the disease had finally claimed her.

"I know, Maryanne," I sobbed, going to her side. "I know."

And then we said nothing. We just cried . . . quietly cried.

Cancer is an insidious disease. It always arrives unannounced, unwanted, and unrelenting. It gnaws at its victim day by day, body part by body part, one hope dashed after another.

In my sister's case, the cancer came on the heels of good news. Her son, my nephew Brandon, had just been declared in remission after some five years of fighting leukemia. He was nine years old when doctors turned their attention to his mom and determined that the pesky lump on her sternum was suspect. The diagnosis rocked the family. We couldn't believe God had penciled all this into His grand plan. It wasn't fair.

Maryanne held out her hand to me. She'd been waiting for months to talk to her youngest brother about dying. Her husband, Eric, and the rest of the family had been maintaining a vigil in my absence.

"I didn't make it, David," she repeated.

I sat down on the bed's edge and leaned over to hug my little sister, making sure I didn't get my hands and arms tangled up in the tubes that carried fluids and medicines into and out of her body. "It's all right. It's all right." We held each other for a minute or two as the heart monitor filled the room with the precious few beats that remained of my sister's life.

And then Maryanne, of all things, apologized. "I tried to be brave."

I pulled her closer. "You *have* been. You still are."

"But I'm so scared."

"I know. I don't think you can be brave *unless* you're scared," I offered. "Only someone stupid wouldn't be scared about dying."

"No, no," said Maryanne, shaking her head back and forth on the pillow. "It's not dying. I'm not afraid of dying."

"You're not?"

"No. I'm afraid of the pain, and mostly, not seeing the

kids grow up, not being their mom, and losing Eric and just . . ."

My sister was thirty-five years old. More than a year earlier, a doctor had misdiagnosed the little lump on her sternum as nothing more than a cyst. When they finally removed it and did a biopsy, they were forced also to remove her breasts. Radiation and chemotherapy followed. A few months later, Maryanne began to experience pain in her right hip. The doctor speculated that it was bursitis—another misdiagnosis.

In June of 1989, Maryanne's brittle right femur broke near the hip. The ambulance came. She screamed with pain. The kids were terrified. The adults were devastated. The doctors said surgery was needed to mend the break.

"At least now," I said to my brother, searching for something positive, "they can go in there and cut the damn cancer out at the same time."

They couldn't do that, of course. The cancer was everywhere. It was advancing like an army sensing the kill. And there was nothing for us to do but hold my sister in our arms, whisper "I love you" over and over, and prepare to let go.

— • —

Irene Weant had spent a year grappling with the reality of letting go. I arrived in Grangeville, Idaho, expecting the interview to result in another slice-of-life story. But Irene greeted me with an unsettling apology.

"This is a rather difficult time for me," she said. "I think my husband is dying today."

Jim Weant was sleeping peacefully at the Sunrise Care Center across town when Irene slipped away to meet me as previously arranged.

"I know, you had no way of knowing," Irene said when I apologized for interfering at such a private time. In fact, when Irene and I talked on the phone the night before she gave no hint of just how grave the situation had become.

"I don't believe in just random things," she explained. "When you called last night, I thought maybe this was ordained . . . and I had something to say about this—if I can get on my soapbox and say, 'You have to tell people today that you love them.' "

Irene, seventy-one, had been making a special effort to tell her husband she loved him ever since he'd fallen months earlier. The accident caused a neck injury that left him a quadriplegic. Able to move his arms only partially, Jim, seventy-three, had spent more than seven months in hospitals. Recently his organs started to fail and he was nearing the end.

"I don't want this worded where it sounds inhumane," Irene cautioned. "Because I've been with this man for fifty-four years and I adore him. But I'm ready to let him go." More important, said Irene, Jim had accepted his own passing.

"If you're going to write a story, I hope you could say something about hope and faith. I stroked his head today and said, 'Maybe today is the day when you go to heaven.' And he said, 'I'll be there waiting for you.' "

The Weants were products of a time when couplehood took precedence over individuality. They met at a USO dance in California near the end of World War II.

"People were still being killed," said Irene. Indeed, her two brothers died overseas. Jim was nineteen and she was seventeen when they were married. "It was a different world. We had war."

Jim, who joined the navy, shipped out soon after the wedding. Irene recalled the endless waiting and the hollow feeling that came with not knowing what was happening in a foreign place where people were dying.

"Every time you got a letter from your loved one, you appreciated it more," she said. When the war ended, Jim came home and the two of them tackled the world together. They raised four daughters while living in California, Texas, and eventually Idaho. The past year, Irene said, was supposed to have been a time of travel and new adventures. Then the accident happened.

"It was just the way he fell," she said of the injury. "My husband has had the most fantastic attitude about this. And I promised him I wouldn't take him to another hospital." Just a couple of weeks earlier, Jim was in the hospital at Cottonwood, Idaho. He'd been at home until taking a turn for the worse. Irene said the family gathered to be at his side. Then Jim rallied and was moved to the care center in Grangeville.

"This last episode in Cottonwood, I saw the drain on him and the punishment he was going through."

So once again, the family came together.

"He's a worrier and he wants to know we'll all be okay. We're all going to just tell him that we love him and will miss him, but that we're going to take care of one another. I told my daughters this morning that I hope I'd taught them how to love. Now I hope I can teach you how to let go. . . . I hope I can show you how to let go of your dad. I want to help them accept death as much as I taught them to live."

A devout Christian, Irene said she'd watched her husband's faith grow over the past year. "What he told me last year is that he hadn't been a Christian up to that point. And he said I want to tell you now that I want your God to be my God."

At one point, Jim lamented that his life had fallen short

of success. She told him nonsense. "I said he'd been a success at everything and if it's time to die, he'll be a success at that too."

I left Irene as she prepared to return to the rest home. We agreed to keep in touch up until press time. Jim held on through the night with his family at his side.

"The vigil of love continues," Irene said as I bid her good night.

The next day, on the day his story appeared in my column, Jim died. Irene had spent the last minutes with him. "I held him in my arms and felt his last breath and his last heartbeat," she said. About one hour before Jim's death, the Weants' fifth granddaughter, Katlin Marie, was born at Grangeville's Syringa Hospital.

Three days later, I attended Jim's funeral. The church was crowded. Everyone marveled at Jim's life and his new-found belief in salvation. I bowed my head when the congregation prayed. . . . "For thine is the kingdom, the power, and the glory, forever and ever. Amen."

It felt good.

— • —

Near the end, ghosts and spirits flitted throughout my sister's hospital room.

"Can't you see them?" she puzzled.

The hallucinations, nurses said, were triggered by the doses of morphine over which Maryanne had control. When the pain was too much, she would simply push a button with her thumb and more liquid drug would flow into her veins, numbing her ravaged body while playing tricks with her mind. She was, in effect, becoming a junkie. It seemed like such an undignified way for such a dignified woman to finish her days.

It didn't seem to bother Maryanne that I couldn't share her visions. She seemed more befuddled than frustrated, almost intrigued by this new, drug-induced world that had become part of the dying process.

I'd taken up residence in Maryanne's room on the oncology floor at the hospital. The nurses moved a cot into the room and I slept for the better part of a week at the foot of my sister's bed, sharing what would become our last days together.

Often I thought of those first words she'd greeted me with: "Oh David, I didn't make it."

Those words will indeed go with me to my own grave someday. Rather than a declaration, they seemed to be more of a pleading from my sister, a last-ditch effort to get her little brother's permission to finally rest after working so hard. Our big brother Bob and I had at times expressed frustration because we couldn't seem to get our sister mad enough to fight the cancer.

By the time Maryanne was admitted to the hospital for the last time, I'd been doing my column for almost six years. I'd already met enough people suffering from a vast array of ailments to know that everyone must approach health problems, and certainly a terminal illness, on their own terms. In my sister's case, I'd pushed the "get tough" routine for more than a year. It was a selfish stance. But finally, there in the hospital room, I tried to imagine her as if she'd simply answered the phone and agreed to talk. Surely I wouldn't have been so bold, if she were a stranger, to think I knew better about her own well-being.

My final acquiescence came on the night of the opening game of the 1989 World Series between the Oakland A's and the San Francisco Giants. Partly, I remember it because Maryanne, an avid Minnesota Twins fan, was anxious to watch the game. And then, of course, there was that terrible Bay Area earthquake that not only postponed the series but also killed hundreds.

More than all that, however, I remember the phone ringing and my sister struggling to reach over and answer it.

"Hello," she said. "Oh, hi, Diane."

My wife was calling from Idaho, probably expecting to hear my voice but getting Maryanne instead. It was, without a doubt, the most extraordinary phone call I've ever listened in on. Even though I heard only my sister's side of the conversation, the essence of what was conveyed between these two women rendered me speechless. They started by discussing not my sister's situation, but the news about the earthquake.

"I feel so sorry for those people," Maryanne said. "It's so sad." She sat almost upright in the hospital bed with pillows stacked behind her back and her bald head. She held the phone with the arm and hand that wasn't weighed down with needles and tubes. The heart monitor beeped in the background as more news about the earthquake filled the television screen. I tried to pay attention as a cameraman focused on baseball great Mark McGwire while he held his child in his arms and looked apprehensively around the stadium.

But then my sister's words began to claim my attention.

"You've been a good sister-in-law too," said Maryanne. "Thank you for everything you and David have done."

Maryanne's eyes seemed to be fixed on the television as she talked. But as I watched and listened, I began to sob like a baby. They were saying good-bye to each other. My wife and my sister were dealing with finality by exchanging only words and the sound of their voices. In my mind, I could see them hugging. And I'm sure they felt the same in their own minds.

"I love you too," Maryanne said. And then she handed

me the phone, turned her head, and began to cry. I put the phone to my ear and heard Diane doing the same.

"I gotta go, babe," I whispered. "I'll call you later."

I spent a couple more days with Maryanne in the hospital before flying home to Idaho again. Oddly enough, I can't remember saying good-bye to her. I just know that she assured me Jesus was at her side and that she was at peace with her passing.

Maryanne died on October 29, 1989, the day before Greta's ninth birthday, and was buried in a new cemetery behind the Lutheran church she and her family attended. She wanted to be there because the only other person in the cemetery was an infant child. Maryanne thought the baby shouldn't be alone.

It's been more than a decade since the funeral. The way I figure it, the time has been filled with well-deserved good fortune for my family back in Minnesota. For the most part, they're healthy in body, mind, and spirit.

— • —

We are, in fact, dying from the day we're born. In a way, the lucky person is the one whose obituary reads "died of causes related to age." There's solace in knowing nothing cut life short.

Debbie LeFors was forced to deal with a different situation entirely. Her husband's death occurred long before it should have. For reasons perhaps not even he fully understood, Dennis LeFors decided on a hot August night that it was time to end it all. He'd been drinking, not only on that day but for years before. His marriage was failing. There were plans for a separation. There was talk of divorce.

Dennis was a mechanic and co-owned an automobile repair shop in Lewiston, Idaho. He liked to fish, hunt, play golf, and bowl. He had two children and by all outward appearances was a typical workaday kind of guy. But inside there was turmoil he could no longer handle. He decided to leave two notes behind. Then he drove his pickup truck home.

Sometime well before sunrise the next morning, Debbie woke with a start to the sound of rock music and her husband's truck idling in the driveway.

"I thought, Oh, my God."

She rushed from bed toward the front door and looked out the window. Amid darkness eased only by streetlights, she could see the truck with a black hose running from the exhaust pipe into the back window of the cab.

"He'd talked about it," wept Debbie, "but I told him there was help available and he agreed with me that getting rid of himself was not an option."

But as Debbie flung open the driver-side door to find her husband of seventeen years slumped in the front seat, the stark reality of Dennis's resolve to commit suicide gave way to her terrified screams for help. Neighbors came running. Emergency crews arrived. Dennis, forty, was taken by ambulance to Saint Joseph Regional Medical Center, where he was pronounced dead of carbon monoxide poisoning.

Just a little over three months after his death, Debbie answered my phone call and we talked about the possibility of an interview. At first the conversation was strained; it almost ended when I apologized for calling during such a difficult time.

"Oh, that's all right," she said.

I knew from my experience in meeting Diane that people sometimes want to talk—maybe even set the public record straight.

"I thought," Debbie said when I arrived the next day at

the LeFors home, "that he'd come to grips with it." Their marriage, she explained, had been undermined for years by her husband's abuse of alcohol. In addition to the two notes, Dennis left behind a ten-year-old son and an eight-year-old daughter. Mostly, Debbie lamented, her husband left lingering forever the question that always begs for an answer: Why?

It was one of the first questions her children asked. At first, she fibbed that their father was sick and had to be taken to the hospital. But she knew the children would eventually demand the truth. "So we sat down and I told them . . . and we all cried and held each other . . . and then came more questions." Debbie said she shared all the details the children wanted to know. "And they pretty much accepted it. They really don't have that many questions now."

As for her own life, Debbie said it had become a day-to-day challenge just to keep looking ahead. "I get a little impatient at times. I haven't really had any close family members die . . . so I've learned a lot about the grieving process." One of the lessons, she said, was not to keep the tragedy locked up inside. She'd been undergoing counseling and was convinced that talking about Dennis's death was necessary to getting on with her own life.

"In the notes, he told me to have a great life. And he told the kids he loved them, and he said he hoped our children would shun alcohol." Debbie said that the stigma of suicide made her husband's death all the worse. If discussed, it was always in hushed tones. "I don't have a problem talking about it because I think there's a lot to learn about it," said Debbie. Much of the mystery about suicide, she suggested, could be understood if friends and relatives of victims simply opened up.

After Debbie's story ran, I discussed it with Diane. "Do you think talking publicly about Stan's death helped you?"

"Sure it did. But you've got to remember, when you interviewed me the story was really about Heidi's being born at home instead of in a hospital. And Stan's death was just part of that story, not *the* story. So I really admire this woman."

"So do I."

Five years passed before I talked again with Debbie. She was still single and going to counseling. I asked her if those years of healing had yielded further insights.

"You know, people tell you it [the grieving] can take up to five years and it definitely does," she said. Her son, who was about to turn fifteen, was also undergoing counseling. "The question of why still bothers him. And he misses his dad." Her daughter seemed to be handling it better than she and her son. The death of a family member from illness, an accident, or aging, said Debbie, is hard enough to handle. "But I really think there's a difference with suicide. Because there is always that question: Why?"

Debbie still owned her husband's 1972 Chevrolet pickup truck. Dennis had taken pride in restoring the truck. "At first I didn't think I'd want it. And then it came to a point where this truck was just the vehicle, so to speak, for his death. But it was also something he loved."

And yes, she said, she still loved Dennis in a way that finally allowed her to both cherish his memory and vent her frustrations. "Angry? Initially, I didn't want to think I had anger in me. But I did. I remember mowing the lawn and saying 'Damn it. Damn you. You leave me with these kids to raise. Damn you. What a responsibility you've left me with. And you're free, or so we think.' "

But with each day, week, month, and year, Debbie said, the anger gave way to acceptance, if not understanding.

She came to the realization that emotional pain is much worse than physical pain. A rational person, she said, "understands that problems are temporary and they can be solved. And you don't have to take a permanent way out."

Her own emotional roller-coaster ride, she confided, was finally leveling out to the point where she could both accept her husband's decision and understand her own feelings of disappointment and frustration. "I've kind of come to the fact that if he was hurting that bad emotionally, then bless his heart. I'm just sorry I couldn't have done something to help."

— • —

As the little genetic time bomb continued to tick, I wished I could do something to help Diane. She had such a big decision to make, the kind more and more people will be faced with as genetic testing becomes a bigger part of medicine.

"If I test negative, then we'll all be home free," said Diane. In addition to learning her own fate, Diane hoped to spare Heidi and Greta of the unknown.

"But if you test positive, then . . ."

"Then they've still got a fifty-fifty chance, but they'd have to get tested themselves to know for sure."

Everything we read about Huntington's suggested the only way the disease can be stopped, short of a medical breakthrough, is for afflicted people not to have children.

"That means, if they knew what we know today," I said, "well, you might not have been born. Or Heidi and Greta . . . if you knew you were a carrier, should you have been sterilized? It all sounds like a horror movie."

"It *is* horrible. But I think not knowing is even more horrible."

So Diane decided it was time to confront the genetic time bomb. As is the case with most medical tests these days, there was an excruciating five-week wait between the time she went in to have blood drawn and when the results came back. The doctor told us we'd have to make another appointment to hear the verdict because she didn't relegate such important matters to a telephone call. So, after six weeks, we were summoned back into the doctor's office. Curiously, Diane's doctor began by making a lot of friendly small talk about my job at the *Tribune* and how much I must enjoy my work.

In retrospect, I knew as soon as the chitchat started that the news was going to be bad. I mean, you don't wait to tell someone they're off the hook. Only when the diagnosis is dire do you pause, hold back, and avoid in hope of lightening the blow.

"Yes, Diane, I'm sorry to say the test came back positive."

"Oh, babe. I'm sorry."

"Well," said Diane, her face flushing red, then going pale, "I kind of had a suspicion."

Silence filled the little office for the next few moments as the doctor, genuinely concerned with our reaction as much as the diagnosis, let the significance of the discovery sink in. The doctor tried to soothe matters by assuring us that Diane was exhibiting no symptoms.

But I later checked out reality on the Internet. "Huntington's disease is an inherited, progressively degenerative neurological disorder that results in the loss of both mental capability and physical control. The ability to think, to speak, and to walk is greatly diminished as the disease progresses."

I stared at the screen, so black and white with its prognosis.

"In the early stages, perhaps even prior to diagnosis,

there is some intellectual, motor, and emotional impairment. With the progression of the disease, the weakened individual succumbs to pneumonia, heart failure, or other complications ultimately resulting in death."

Then, in bold print with three exclamation points: "Presently, there is no effective treatment or known cure!!!"

CONCLUSION

A New Day

The sun rises right outside our dining room window here on Hatter Creek. Dawn always makes me wish I were more of a morning person. Abiding by nighttime deadlines isn't conducive to rising early. So I envy farmers and loggers and others of more diurnal professions who're almost always up to experience the wonders of daybreak.

Sometimes, when the night air chills my bones and the stove demands stoking, I manage to wake early and make my way downstairs in a sleepy fog. I'm jolted by the orange globe that sends shafts of new light across the ground and through the window. We all face the same sun each morning. And this, I think, is what we all live for—the prospect of happiness that comes with a new day. We savor the past and relish the present, but we can dream only of the future. And with a dream comes hope, that inner quest for fulfillment that drives human beings.

I stand shivering while the rekindled stove resumes its duel with the cold innards of our home, wondering what it would be like if tomorrow the sun didn't rise. Maybe for the rest of the world, it would rise. But what if it didn't come

---

up for me or someone close to me, like Diane, who's still sleeping under the down comforter upstairs? I think of her and covet the prospect of falling in love over and over again.

As I get older, I like to walk the half-mile to the bottom of the driveway and get the paper, especially if it's Friday and my column is on the front page. The *Trib* always arrives around daybreak. When people ask about my favorite column, I say, "Next week's is my favorite." I like the mystery that comes with not knowing who'll answer my call. I like the idea of scrolling down those pages of names with my finger and stopping to touch the next person's life.

But if I really had to look back and choose someone who embodies what "Everyone Has a Story" has meant to me, it would be Vera Morris.

When I interviewed Vera way back in 1984, she mixed the drinks and I proposed a toast. To her.

"Thank you." She smiled.

The ice tinkled in our glasses. The whiskey was smooth.

"I'm hoping this interview will help someone else," said Vera, adjusting herself behind her aluminum walker and shuffle-stepping back to the table. "Otherwise, when you called I would have told you to forget it."

I scratched her words in my notebook and took another swallow as Vera reached toward a tape player before sitting down.

"Music?" she queried. "I prefer semi-classical. May I put some on for you?"

Placido Domingo's voice soon filled Vera's home. I thought it was "pretty."

"That's *beautiful*," she corrected.

Vera lived alone in a little house in the Orchards neighborhood of Lewiston, Idaho, with a white cat named Twit and a sunroom full of plants. At fifty-seven, she'd learned to compensate for misfortune by refusing to let anything take the smile from her face. Injuries had left her propped behind the walker, and sometimes, she confided, her circumstances required a stiff drink.

"I'm just a woman who's living alone and getting around with a walker," said Vera, condensing her story into one sentence. Before I made more of her situation than warranted, Vera preempted any questions that might smack of pity.

"I can't do too much, but I keep pushing," she declared. "Might as well take a pistol to your head . . . if you don't keep trying."

I'll drink to that, I thought, lifting my glass and offering Vera another silent toast.

It was almost ten years earlier that the walker had become part of Vera's days. "This is the rest of my life," she said, gripping the cold metal stand. "I figure I just have to accept it." First a back injury, then a series of broken legs caused permanent damage—slowing Vera's body, but not her spirit.

"Nothing stops me. I just keep going."

While we talked, a pair of wind chimes just outside the window competed with Placido Domingo. Vera called the chimes Thor and Deep Throat. One was pitched high, the other low. Together, explained Vera, they tattled whenever the wind misbehaved.

Then, winking through her glass of whiskey on the rocks, Vera tattled about herself. There was a man in her life.

"Let's just call him My Friend. He's a good friend. But he doesn't want his name mentioned. I help him, and he helps me."

My Friend was responsible for most of her surroundings, said Vera. "He went around here today picking up and made sure everything was up to perfection because you were coming."

Born in neighboring Clarkston, Washington, Vera spent some time in California but had lived in the Lewiston area most of her life. Divorced, she had no children.

"But I love plants and animals," said Vera, stroking Twit's silky coat and beginning to recite the names of the many plants hanging in her sunroom.

"Palm tree, velvet plant, Moses in the cradle, cat's whiskers, bridal veil, spider plant, artillery plant, weeping fig," the list continued. "I love them all. This is my life," Vera said, setting her drink aside and lifting her arms in a sweeping motion around the room.

About that time, Twit stood up in her lap and hopped down.

"No, you're not going outside. Get on that chair, now—move it," Vera commanded the cat. Like a furry robot, Twit did just that, springing up into a chair near me.

I marveled at a cat that actually minded her owner's orders.

"She hears me," Vera said. Within moments, Twit was back in her lap, soaking up any affection offered while Vera got back to talk of plants.

The key to growing healthy plants—"and maybe our own health"—said Vera, is music. "This goes day and night," she said, cocking an ear toward Placido Domingo as he crooned strains to "Perhaps Love."

"I believe in giving plants music," she said. "It's the vibrations in the air."

Vera confided that, like a plant, she could just wither away on the vine and let the day's problems close in. She could shut the doors to newspaper reporters and the rest of the world. But she refused to extend loneliness an invitation.

"Plants, embroidery work . . . anything. Just do something instead of stagnate," she advised.

A commotion rose at the door. Twit jumped down. Vera directed her attention away from me, then announced that My Friend had returned unexpectedly. A gregarious sort, he gave me his first name, "but not for print."

Among the many things My Friend had done for Vera was giving her a worry stone, a chunk of hardwood about softball size.

"When I get nervous or anything I rub that thing," Vera laughed as we all settled into idle conversation that felt, well, as soothing as a smooth liqueur. More than an hour passed. I finally finished my drink. Vera was still nursing hers. My Friend wasn't drinking. Twit was still purring.

"There's no way they're going to keep me down," Vera said.

Ten years after Vera and I tipped a couple, I paid another visit. She'd moved to an even smaller trailer. She still sipped whiskey, smoked cigarettes, and unwittingly paid me the best compliment I've ever had as a reporter.

"Here, look," she said. "I still have it."

From out of her wallet Vera pulled a clipping of the original column I wrote about her.

I thought that was amazing.

"Not really," she corrected.

Vera was still getting around with the same aluminum walker, but confessed that without help from a nursing aide she might be in a rest home. Deep Throat, the wind chime, continued to hang outside her doorway. Twit was now living in the country with some of Vera's friends. Placido Domingo's music still filled her life. Many of her old plants, the ones I'd met a decade earlier, were still growing strong.

But My Friend had died two years earlier.

"I'm sorry."

"Thank you," she whispered.

Then I reached over and took the old newspaper clipping in my hand. It was yellowed and ragged along the edges and some of the words were hard to read where she'd folded it into her wallet. I gave Vera a hug. Then she poured two more drinks and we toasted friendship.

"To you," she said.

"No," I corrected. "To you, Vera."

Sometimes I look back at my interviews with people like Vera and think it's time to be a philanthropist. I wish I could better share my good fortune. I wish I could divvy up my experiences, as have all the people who've parceled out their stories to me.

If we're shaped by experience, then part of everyone I've interviewed has become part of me, and I've become a part of their lives too. I can only hope I've given these people a fair shake in handling their stories. If I could borrow just one of their character traits, it would be resilience—their ability to cope with difficulty and look forward to the dawn of a new day.

Diane is doing that now. To date, she's shown no perceptible symptoms. She knows that the onset of Huntington's varies with individuals. And that gives her hope. But she also knows that it's only a matter of time before the disease takes hold. So she tries to tighten her own hold on what she loves most: her daughters, family, home, friends, pets, and me.

"I'm just thankful for every day I don't have symptoms," she says. She also hopes aloud about science rescuing her. Most of all, she tells me that she wants to savor the life that remains for us.

"I want to live it one day at a time."

To the uninitiated—those who haven't had to tap a personal reservoir of strength—Diane's words may sound both maudlin and trite. But they echo true in my ears. I've heard them so many times from people I've met through the phone book. While listening, I've wondered why they agreed, like Diane did so long ago, to tell their stories to a stranger who, in turn, tells thousands of others. The only thing I can come up with is that these people have experienced enough triumphs to share both their victories *and* their defeats. Think about that. What more could we ask of ourselves?

I've seen Diane continue to triumph. In a way, the Huntington's diagnosis was a blessing. If she hadn't gone ahead with the test she'd still have the possibility of the disease hanging over her head. Oh sure, blissful ignorance might have spared her a certain kind of worry. But she doesn't worry now as much as she *prepares*. And the preparation, while dealing with what is probably inevitable, mostly focuses on embracing what she already has in her life. For example, we've pared back on the dog-kennel business so she can pursue other interests, like spending more time with her family and friends.

As for our daughters, Heidi and Greta know they're at risk and that testing, especially if they plan to have a family, might be in the offing. Diane is confident that research will intervene with a treatment or a cure before they get old enough to develop symptoms. Like their mom, the girls cling to that hope and keep moving ahead.

These days Heidi lives in Boise and works as a cosmetologist. Hopeful of owning her own salon in a few years, she cuts Mom's and Dad's hair whenever we visit Boise or she ventures "home."

Greta attends Washington State University, runs on the cross-country and track teams there, and has set her sights on veterinary school. Ever since childhood, she's wanted to care for sick animals, "even sharks."

And what about me? I suspect I'll always be looking at the dawn in search of rhyme and reason. But I'm also reveling in what I can only describe as good fortune. I'm surrounded by my family and the land we love so much. I'm looking forward to getting a couple new company cars over the next decade and roving the same beat that never gets old. I'm ecstatic that in late 1997 Butch Alford managed to gather up the financial wherewithal to buy the *Tribune* back. The purchase triggered much celebrating in the newsroom; and later that day, a vast sense of relief when I came home to announce, "We have a job!"

And I always have the phone book with all those names and numbers. If everyone indeed has a story, then mine has become inescapably intertwined with the people whose stories I've told. Over the better part of two decades, these people have confirmed the notion that everyone is worthy of the front page. Moreover, they've shown me how to appreciate the simple things we already have within our grasp and the exhilaration that comes with looking ahead—like to the next person who answers a random call.

A newspaper's headline might feature a jet that crashes, but I think the *truly* important news is that all the other planes routinely take off and land. Sometimes the most important lessons are found not at the pinnacle of what we consider news, but amid the routine ups and downs experienced by everyday people. Epiphanies will always be elusive. Most of the answers to life's riddles hide not in the profound, but in the ordinary; not in the unusual, but in the conventional; not in the celebrity pages of a newspaper, but perhaps in the white pages of a phone book.

I'll never forget that night long ago in the *Tribune*'s newsroom when I found Marciano Prado's name at the tip of my finger. I also think back warmly to that blustery day in 1976 with Leo Koch in the Cavendish Store. I can still hear the creak of the wooden floor under my feet, the hush of the Chinook wind brushing against the old building, and that little voice whispering in my head, *Everyone has a story.*